MW01169453

SERVICENOW DEVELOPMENT HANDBOOK

Third Edition

A compendium of pro-tips, guidelines, and best practices for ServiceNow developers, Administrators, and Architects

Tim Woodruff

Dedicated to:

Roger, Ciel, Bill, and Casey.

Lily, Ozy, and the King family.

You – for reading.
Thank you.

OH, and my dog: Ezri Dax.
She's super cute. You should definitely follow her on Instagram:
@ThreeLegger

Tim Woodruff

Version 3.0

If you've purchased this book on Kindle, you can check for updates and ensure that you have the latest version of this edition for free by going to http://update.snc.guru/.

Tim Woodruff

*Also dedicated to the entire **ServiceNow development community**, and everyone who takes time out of their day to help other administrators, developers, and architects learn the ins-and-outs of the massively feature-rich ServiceNow platform.*

The (unofficial) ServiceNow community Discord and Slack servers are full of the most helpful and supportive people I know. If you're not a member, stop by and say hi!

Special thanks to technical and content editors:

Robert Fedoruk
https://theduke.digital

Paul McNamara
https://pamtconsulting.com

And thanks to all the readers who wrote in to contribute.

CONTENTS

ABOUT THE AUTHOR

TIM WOODRUFF has worked in IT for over 15 years, and has written software for even longer. For the past several years, Tim has narrowed his focus to ServiceNow's IT Service Management platform, otherwise known as the "Now" platform. He continues to work with several companies as an independent consultant to help implement and manage ServiceNow instances.

Tim has written multiple books on ServiceNow's "NOW" platform (which you can find at http://books.snc.guru/), and writes a ServiceNow development blog that's full of tips, tricks, best-practices, and free ServiceNow tools (http://snprotips.com/).

Tim is a huge nerd. He enjoys reading sci-fi and non-fiction, as well as listening to audiobooks, studying physics and programming, discussing philosophy, exploring ghost towns, and going on long road-trip adventures with his drone and three-legged dog, Ezri.

You can find Tim on LinkedIn at https://www.linkedin.com/in/sn-timw/, on Twitter at @TheTimWoodruff, or at his developer blog: http://snprotips.com/.

INTRODUCTION

BEING A SERVICENOW ARCHITECT with a technical training background, I often find myself teaching development and administration standards and best-practices in ServiceNow, as well as why those best-practices are important. Having a complete understanding of why a given standard is what it is (and why it's important), will not only make people more likely to adhere to it, but will empower them to apply the underlying concepts elsewhere, and make them more effective administrators, developers, or architects. That's the spirit in which The ServiceNow Development Handbook was written: A spirit of teaching and explaining, not simply listing out a series of edicts under the heading of "best-practice" without further explanation.

This is a condensed "developer guide", not a complete ServiceNow training course in book-form. It assumes that you're already at least somewhat familiar with the ServiceNow platform, and that you already have at least a working knowledge of JavaScript.

If you don't yet know much about ServiceNow, consider reading another of my books to get up to speed: **Learning ServiceNow, Second Edition** (*ISBN-13: 978-1788837040*) which you can find at the URL http://lsn.snc.guru/.

If you have a basic understanding of **the ServiceNow** platform and **JavaScript**, I hope you'll think of this book as your roadmap to making your work in ServiceNow clean, effective, safe, and robust.

Keep in mind that these are **guidelines**. For virtually every rule in this compendium, there is probably at least one exception. What is important, is **understanding** when you're deviating from best-practice and **having a good reason for it**. Better yet, **documenting** that reason so any developers who come after you don't have to guess!

An example where best practice isn't always possible or ideal is DOM (Document Object Model) manipulation. "Best practice" is clear that this should be avoided as it is not well supported, and is vulnerable to collisions with future versions. This happened when Service Portal was released and broke most, if not all, DOM access. This resulted in a great deal of problems when client-side scripts which made use of DOM manipulation did not work when pages, catalog items, or forms were rendered in the Service Portal.

There will be cases where you try all the alternatives and can't find a better way to accomplish a business-critical change. In these cases, it is always wise to consult your ServiceNow technical architect or fellow developers first, to see if there might be a better way. (You can find great developer communities on Slack and Discord, both linked to in the "Contact" menu on https://SNProTips.com/). Sometimes a better way cannot be found. This is okay! Just remember to document that you tried, and to have (and document) a good reason for the exception.

Code snippets and examples featured in this book are available on Github so you can review them in more detail and copy/paste them into your development instance. The code can be found at https://handbook3code.snc.guru/.

Note: If you find any errors or omissions in this book, please get in touch with me! You can reach me any time via Twitter (@TheTimWoodruff) where my DMs are typically open, or on LinkedIn at https://www.linkedin.com/in/sn-timw/.

Your journey begins.

CODE & CODING GUIDELINES

Hello, World!

Always code as if the guy who ends up maintaining
your code will be a violent psychopath who knows
where you live.
—Martin Golding

First, solve the problem. Then, write the code.
—John Johnson

We use JavaScript to interact with ServiceNow, using the Glide API. We even use JavaScript in *server-side* scripts; even though ServiceNow runs on Mozilla Rhino (a Java–based implementation of JavaScript). As with any large platform, there are certain standards and guidelines that we should do our best to follow, in order to avoid pitfalls and make sure we're building resilient functionality. In this chapter, we're going to learn about some best practices for coding with the Glide API, and using JavaScript in ServiceNow (and in general). We'll learn how to avoid common pitfalls and write clear, consistent code we can be proud of!

PURE FUNCTIONS

Pure functions are functions which do not rely on the state of any code except their own. No matter what else is going on in the parent scope of a *pure* function, as long as the same data is passed into it, it will always return the same result. Pure functions are much easier to understand than functions that rely on state, and they tend to be much more modular as well. You don't *always* have to use pure functions, but it's *almost always* a good idea.

(As with all of these guidelines, use your best judgement.)

When calling a pure function with the same argument values, it always produces the same output, regardless of the state of the rest of the environment or calling scope. This means the function should not have any unpredictable side-effects or rely on state data — such as time, object properties, data in the calling scope, other variables (ones not passed in as arguments), etc.

The following function **uses**, but does not **declare**, a variable called myName. It requires that a global (or parent-scope) variable called myName be declared elsewhere, and is therefore **not** a pure function:

```
function sayHello() {
  alert('Hello, ' + myName + '!');
}
```
Fig. 1.01: An impure function

However, if we pass in myName whenever this function is called – even if we expect this always to be the same value – we make the function much easier to read, update, and repurpose. This is what **pure** functions are all about!

```
function sayHello(myName) {
  alert('Hello, ' + myName + '!');
}
```
Fig. 1.02: A pure function

A common example of a **non-pure function**, is a Script Include with a method (a function inside the Script Include class) which is meant to be called from within a Business Rule. The Business Rule contains the current variable; and yes, technically, the Script Include (when called from the Business Rule) *can* access that variable, without it being passed in as an argument. But what if the functionality of that method needs to be re-used from a different script, in a different context? If you pass the current variable in as an argument instead, then it can accept any GlideRecord as an argument, and won't be dependent on the exact scope from which it was called!

WRITING DRY CODE

DRY:
   Don't
   Repeat
   Yourself

DRY is a common saying among experienced programmers and is a good standard to code by. It means that in *almost* all situations, you should avoid **duplicating** a block of code over and over, even if the duplicate blocks all vary in some small way.

There is almost always a better way to code.

Often, the better way involves constructing an **object** or **array** of objects with some representation of the data that differ between each block of code, and then looping over those properties to perform the same operation with each set of data.

Consider the following code:

```
var grIncident = new GlideRecord('incident');
var encodedQuery = 'some_encoded_query_here';
grIncident.addEncodedQuery(encodedQuery);
grIncident.query();
while (grIncident.next()) {
   grIncident.setValue('state', 3); //Set state to work in
progress
   grIncident.update();
}

//lather, rinse, repeat
var grProblem = new GlideRecord('problem');
var encodedQuery = 'some_encoded_query_here';
grProblem.addEncodedQuery(encodedQuery);
grProblem.query();
while (grProblem.next()) {
   grProblem.setValue('state', 4); //set state to some
other state
   grProblem.update();
}

//lather, rinse, repeat
var grChange = new GlideRecord('change_request');
```

```
var encodedQuery = 'some_encoded_query_here';
grChange.addEncodedQuery(encodedQuery);
grChange.query();
while (grChange.next()) {
  grChange.setValue('state', 5); //always specify what
the integer corresponds to when setting state
  grChange.update();
}
//[and so on…]
```

Fig. 1.03: Inefficiently written, non-"DRY" code

This code does the **same thing** multiple times, with only very minor differences in functionality each time. The only differences between each chunk of code are highlighted in bold: the table name, the query, and the state value.

This type of code is inefficient to write, hard to read, and prone to errors. Imagine if you needed to make a change to the way this runs. You'd need to change it in **three** (or more) places, just to make **one** change. With that many changes being necessary, there's also a good chance that you or someone who comes after you, will make a mistake. You'll then end up with a bug that only occurs conditionally and is thus much more difficult to troubleshoot.

Hopefully I've made the point by now, that "DRY" code is preferable to, uh… wet code? – That is, code which repeats itself. – Now that we know what *not* to do, how do we write our code more efficiently and effectively? Instead of repeating the entire code block, we could construct an array of objects which contain the data that constitutes the differences between each of the code blocks (highlighted in bold in the code above). Once we've got that data, we can simply iterate through it and use the values in each object. Here is an example of one way this may be done:

```
var i,
    grRecord,
    stateChange,
    stateChangeDetails = [ //An array of objects
        {
            table_name : 'incident',
            encoded_query : 'some_query',
            state_value : 3
        },
        {
            table_name : 'problem',
            encoded_query : 'some_other_query',
            state_value : 4
        },
        {
            table_name : 'change_request',
            encoded_query : 'yet_a_third_query',
            state_value : 5
        }
```

```
    ];

for (i = 0; i < stateChangeDetails.length; i++) {
    stateChange = stateChangeDetails[i];
    grRecord = new GlideRecord(stateChange.table_name);
    grRecord.addEncodedQuery(stateChange.encoded_query);
    grRecord.query();
    while (grRecord.next()) {
//set state to work in progress
        grRecord.setValue('state',
stateChange.state_value);
        grRecord.update();
    }
}
```

Fig. 1.04: Better, DRYer code, with room for improvement

The above code is **much** more effective, and "**DRY**". However, there's an even better (or at least, more efficient) way to do this: by using constructors!

Constructors (in JavaScript **ES5**, which ServiceNow's application server[1] runs) are functions which are called along with the **new** keyword, to "construct" an object with the properties specified. Here's a very simple example of a **constructor** function:

```
function Person(name, age, coolness) {
    this.name = name;
    this.age = age;
    this.coolness = coolness;
}
```

Fig. 1.05: A simple constructor (in JavaScript ES5)

Note: *This function name (*`Person()`*) begins with a capital **P**. Unlike normal functions in JavaScript[2], constructors should always have names beginning with a **capital** letter.*

---

[1] *ServiceNow's "application server" is where your **server-side code** runs. Client-side code executes inside the user's browser, but anything that runs server-side runs on the application server, which runs Mozilla Rhino: a Java-based implementation of JavaScript.*

Until more recent versions of ServiceNow, the application server only supported ES3. A few years ago though, ServiceNow updated the version of Mozilla Rhino that it was running on its application servers, to a version which supported ES5. It will still probably be a while though, before we're able to run ES6 JavaScript server-side in ServiceNow.

[2] ***Note:** **Java** is to **JavaScript** as "**Car**" is to "**Carpet**": effectively unrelated! You and I may understand this, but recruiters often don't. If you put the term "JavaScript" in your profile, prepare to be spammed by recruiters looking for a "Java" developer.*

This function sets local-scope properties **name**, **age**, and **coolness**, to the values that were passed in (using the `this`[3] object, like `"this.prop_name"`). We do not need to return anything, since the `new` keyword takes care of this for us[4]. We can construct a new object using this constructor function like so:

```
var personMe = new Person('Tim', 32, 'Extreme to the
max');
```
Fig. 1.06: Initializing a variable to a new object, using a constructor

In the preceding line, I pass in `'Tim'` for the name, `30` for the age, and `'Extreme to the max'` for the coolness. The resulting object looks like this, when printed to the console:

```
Person {name: "Tim", age: 30, coolness: "Extreme to the max"}
  age: 30
  coolness: "Extreme to the max"
  name: "Tim"
```

It is often useful to know what constructor was used to create a given object. You can find this out, by accessing the `.constructor.name` property, like so: `someObject.constructor.name`.

In the preceding example, that would be **personMe**`.constructor.name`, since personMe is a reference to our object. That would return the string "Person".

Note: I've named the variable `personMe`, *because – as we'll learn in the* ***Naming Conventions*** *section of this book, it's a good idea to try to give some indication as to an object's* ***type*** *in its name, so you'll have an easier time remembering what it contains when you see it again a hundred lines later without context. This is why you'll see me use variable names beginning with* ***"gr"*** *(such as* `grIncident`) *for GlideRecords.*

---

[3] *The "`this`" object in JavaScript always refers to the function it is in. In JavaScript, functions are just a special type of object. Thus,* `this.prop_name` *sets references the* `prop_name` *property of the object that you'll end up with when you call a constructor with the new keyword.*

[4] *The* `new` *keyword in JavaScript can be used with a* ***constructor*** *function, which sets properties of the* `this` *object, which is then effectively "returned" (though no* `return` *statement is necessary; the* `new` *keyword takes care of that when it's called). It can be used like so:*

```
var myObject = new SomeConstructorFunction(args);
```
Fig. 1.07: Generalized constructor invocation

You can read more in the Mozilla JavaScript documentation:
https://developer.mozilla.org/en-US/docs/Web/JavaScript/Reference/Operators/new

Of course, a constructor is a **function**, so you can add some fancy code into it like any other function! For example, you can set a default value[5] for a property, or do some validation, as in the following code:

```
function Person(name, age, coolness) {
    this.name = name ? name : 'Bob'; //Default to Bob if
falsey value was passed in
    this.age = Number(age); //Cast age to a number
    this.coolness = function(coolness) { //self-executing
function to validate coolness value
    var actualCoolness = 'Total doof';
    if (coolness === actualCoolness) {
        return coolness;
    } else {
        return actualCoolness;
    }
}(); //Adding "()" makes it an IIFE, which executes and
returns the value, instead of setting the coolness
property to the function itself.


var personMe = new Person('', '30', 'Extreme to the max');
```
Fig. 1.08: Constructor creation and usage example

The `personMe` object will then look something like this:

```
▼ Person {name: "Bob", age: 30, coolness: "Total doof"} ⓘ
    age: 30
    coolness: "Total doof"
    name: "Bob"
```

You can also do other neat things with constructors, like **override** properties, **validate** values, set **default** property values, **add** "*methods*" (functions contained within the objects generated from the constructor), and fun stuff like that. To read more, check out the Mozilla JS docs; but remember that ServiceNow server-side code cannot run ES6 JavaScript (AKA: ECMAScript 2015). It can only process **ES5** code.:

https://developer.mozilla.org/en-US/docs/Web/JavaScript/Reference/Operators/new

Now that we understand **constructors** in JavaScript, let's revisit the example earlier in this chapter. As a reminder, here's the example we left off with:

---

[5] *For more on setting default values for function parameters, see the **Modularity** > **Default Function Parameters** section of the **Configurability** chapter in this book. There, we also cover the concept of "ternary operators", which the function below uses. If it doesn't make sense to you yet, don't worry, it will.*

```
    new StateChangeDetail('incident', 'some_query', 3),
    new StateChangeDetail('problem', 'some_other_query',
4),
    new StateChangeDetail('change_request', 'third_query',
5)
];

for (i = 0; i < stateChangeDetails.length; i++) {
    stateChange = stateChangeDetails[i];
    grRecord = new GlideRecord(stateChange.table_name);
    grRecord.addEncodedQuery(stateChange.encoded_query);
    grRecord.query();

    while (grRecord.next()) {
        grRecord.setValue('state',
stateChange.state_value);
        grRecord.update();
    }
}
```

Fig. 1.10: Quite optimized and DRY code, using what we've learned

In the above code (on *line* 7), we declare our constructor, which takes three arguments: `table`, `query`, and `state`. From those, it constructs an object with three properties: `table_name`, `encoded_query`, and `state_value`. Then, on *lines 13-17*, we build an array of objects generated from that constructor, using the `new` keyword.

Finally, we loop over the array, and access the elements of the objects to do the work we need to do.

The above code is pretty *DRY* and quite effective. However, we have one more alternative way of writing this, which is my personal favorite by far: We can write it **functionally**. That is, we can do this work by using a function which we can call and simply pass in the data that it would need to do this work. Rather than building an array of objects that contain the data we need, we can just pass them into a helper function as arguments! This also allows us to do some neat stuff, like having an **optional** argument – making the encoded query optional allows the calling code to not specify a query at all, thus updating all records in the table.

Here is what the updated code looks like:

```
changeState('incident', 3, 'some_query');
changeState('problem', 4, 'some_other_query');
changeState('change_request', 5, 'third_query');
```

```
 * @param {string} tableName - The name of the table to run
this operation against
 * @param {string|number} newState - The new value for the
state field. This may be an integer or string, depending
on the value expected by the table provided.
 * @param {string} [encodedQuery] - A string containing the
encoded query to filter the records on which to perform
this operation. If no query is provided, ALL records in
the table will be modified.
 * @return {number} - The number of records on which this
operation was performed.
 */
function changeState(tableName, newState, encodedQuery) {
   var grRecord = new GlideRecord(tableName);
   if (encodedQuery) {
       grRecord.addEncodedQuery(encodedQuery);
   }

   grRecord.setValue('state', newState); //set state to
work in progress
   grRecord.updateMultiple();

   return grRecord.getRowCount();
}
```

Fig. 1.11: Highly optimized, DRY, _and_ "functional" code[6]

Note: In this script, I've also made use of the `updateMultiple()` GlideRecord API, which should make things even more efficient! For more information, you can check out my article on updateMultiple() and deleteMultiple(), at http://multiops.snc.guru/.

PASS-BY-REFERENCE

One thing to note about dealing with functions, scope, and objects in general in JavaScript, is an oddity of the language called **pass-by-reference**, or PBR. PBR is not unique to JavaScript, but is something that you might not run into in a lot of other languages, especially those that are "strictly typed" (where variables are declared with, and must remain, one specific data-type).

Following, is probably one of the **most important guidelines** in this book, yet it might also be one of the **least adhered-to**. When I want to know if someone really has a firm understanding of JavaScript, knowledge of pass-by-reference is one of the things that I look for (among other things, like scope, closure, and the `this` object).

---

[6] Note that on line 21 in the above code, we use .getRowCount(). This particular method of the GlideRecord class is actually quite performance-intensive, and should be avoided if at all possible, for code that needs to be remotely efficient.

Consider the following code:

```
var coolness = 'Extreme to the max';
changeCoolness(coolness);
console.log(coolness);

function changeCoolness(coolness) {
  var actualCoolnessLevel = 'Total doofus';
  coolness = actualCoolnessLevel;
}
```

Fig. 1.12: Passing and mutating[7] a string[8] without returning it

In this code, I'm declaring my coolness to be **Extreme to the max** on *line 1*, but since I *probably* shouldn't rely on my mom's opinion as the objective measure of my coolness, I pass `coolness` into a function called `changeCoolness()`, which modifies the variable we've passed into it, and sets it to my *actual* coolness level. This function does not return a value, it simply modifies the `coolness` variable, and then ends.

Since the value we passed into this function is a **primitive** (a *string, number, or Boolean*), passing it into the `changeCoolness()` function creates a **new variable** with a **copy** of the value from the `coolness` variable, in the scope of the `changeCoolness()` function. Because of this, when we print out the value of `coolness` on *line 3*, we see that the value has **not actually changed**. Despite being modified in the scope of the `changeCoolness()` function, the value that prints out on *line 3* is still "**Extreme to the max**". In other words, the variable is not modified "in-place[9]".

Note: *Even if we were to* `return` *a value from this function, that would not alter the behavior discussed below, since we're not* using *that returned value.*

---

[7] *To "mutate" a variable pretty much just means to change it. We coders sure do like to use five-dollar words for simple concepts sometimes, don't we?*

Technically, "mutate" may refer to altering the actual value, or simply the nature of the data in a variable; but you can usually safely think of the word "mutate" as meaning "change in some way".

[8] *Two footnotes in the same sentence? Does that mean I'm doing something very right, or very wrong? – Anyway, technically, "primitive" datatypes in JavaScript (strings, booleans, and numbers) are "immutable", meaning that rather than modifying the actual data in memory when we assign a new primitive value to a variable, a new "instance" of the variable's data is created. The actual implications of that fact are… well, very little to you; but I knew that if I didn't point it out, I'd get at least a half dozen angry emails the day this book came out.*

[9] *To modify a variable "**in-place**" means to pass it into some function or otherwise access it from outside the scope in which it's declared, but to then modify its value in a way that impacts the calling scope. Passing an object into a function and then modifying the variable which contains that object in that function, will modify the object "in-place", meaning that it'll be modified as well, in the scope from which it was passed into the function which modified it.*

If you find that explanation to be about as clear as a glass of Flint Michigan tap water, you can find a more detailed write-up at: http://pbr.snc.guru/

If we were to modify line 2 in the above code, to instead read `coolness = changeCoolness(coolness);` ***and*** *return the new value of coolness,* **only then** *would the function result in the value of the* `coolness` *variable being altered* <u>outside</u> *the function.*

This is likely how you would expect this code to behave. However, for **non-primitive** variable types, this code would behave in almost exactly **the opposite** way!

First, let's just clarify what **non-primitive** values are: A non-primitive value is essentially anything that isn't a *string, boolean, number,* `null`, or `undefined`. *Anything* that isn't one of those five data-types, is technically an **Object**. This includes *objects* (obviously), *arrays, functions, prototypes,* and lots of other types of stuff. The following object, called `me`, is an example of a **non-primitive** value. (There's nothing special about it that makes it non-primitive; **all** objects are non-primitive.)

```
var me = {
  name : 'Tim',
  age : 30,
  coolness : 'Extreme to the max'
};
```
Fig. 1.13: Declaring an object with various properties, representing a person.

Let's take our code from the previous example (which you'll recall did **not** modify the `coolness` variable in-place), and let's try the same thing using the above non-primitive **object**. Here's *that* code:

```
var me = {
  name : 'Tim',
  age : 30,
  coolness : 'Extreme to the max'
};

changeCoolness(me);
console.log('I\'m this cool: ' + me.coolness);

function changeCoolness(person) {
  var actualCoolnessLevel = 'Total doofus';
  person.coolness = actualCoolnessLevel;
}
```
Fig. 1.14: Mutating an object; altering the value of one of its properties

Consider the above code carefully. What do you think will happen when we print out the value of the coolness property on *line 8*?

You may be surprised to find that even though the only place where the value was changed was in the scope of the function (which never returned a value), the updated string "**Total doofus**" will print out!

```
> var me = {
      name : 'Tim',
      age : 30,
      coolness : 'Extreme to the max'
  };

  changeCoolness(me);
  console.log('I\'m this cool: ' + me.coolness);

  function changeCoolness(person) {
      var actualCoolnessLevel = 'Total doofus';
      person.coolness = actualCoolnessLevel;
  }

  I'm this cool: Total doofus ◄──────
```

This is because when we passed the argument `me` into the `changeCoolness()` function, we actually passed a **reference** to the object. That means that the variable `person` in the function, and the variable `me` in the parent scope, both literally *refer* to the **same object** in memory!

I don't mean that both variables "contain an object with the same value"; I mean they both contain a reference to *literally* the same object. Whatever you do to one variable, you do to the other, because they are *literally* referring to *the same object*.

(Am I saying the word "literally" too much?)

This has major implications for how your code functions, both for abstract objects, and for doing things like working with `GlideRecord` and `GlideElement` objects; especially when working within <u>loops</u> which may modify or access some property of an object. It is not "incorrect" to use either **pass-by-reference** (with *objects, functions,* etc.), or **pass-by-value** (with *primitives*), but it *is* important to **understand the differences in behavior**.

More information on this concept, and a helpful article with more examples, can be found in the section **Getting and setting field values**.

Pro-tip. *You can find lots more info including a deep-dive on this topic, at http://pbr.snc.guru/!*

GETTING AND SETTING FIELD VALUES

When working with **GlideRecord** objects, it's common to either get or set the value of a specific field. To do that, it's important to use a **getter** (`.getValue()`) and **setter** (`.setValue()`). This section explains why and how to do that, in more detail. The important takeaway is to avoid using notation like `gr.field_name` which directly accesses the **GlideElement** object for the field (though there are some **exceptions**, such as Journal fields). Every field in a **GlideRecord** object (whether it's "`current`" in a Business Rule, or a variable you've declared like "`grIncident`" in a Script Include) is itself, another **object**; a type of object called a **GlideElement**. So, with that in mind, consider the following code:

```
var shortDesc = grInc.short_description;
```
Fig. 1.15: Setting a variable (shortDesc) to a **reference** to an object

In the preceding line of code, I'm actually setting the variable `shortDesc` to a **reference** to the **GlideElement**[10] object located at `grInc.short_description`. If that value changes, so does your variable, because JavaScript uses **pass-by-reference** (PBR); and remember, every time you call `.next()` (for example, `grInc.next()`), it changes the values in every GlideElement/"field" on your GlideRecord object!

Note: More on PBR in the previous section (Pass-by-Reference), or in my "SN Pro Tips" article at http://pbr.snc.guru/).

For this reason, we should virtually always use the `.getValue()` method of GlideRecord objects to retrieve a value, and `.setValue()` to set a value.
There are three main exceptions to this:

1. **Journal fields**[11]
   a. To interact with a journal field, just access it directly (e.g. `current.work_notes = 'note';`).

2. **Catalog variables**

---

[10] Documentation on the GlideElement class of objects is available on https://developer.servicenow.com/ Scoped GlideElement API docs (as of Orlando):
https://developer.servicenow.com/dev.do#!/reference/api/orlando/server/no-namespace/c_GlideElementScopedAPI
[11] Journal fields and catalog variables are different because they "contain" (or rather, **relate to**) values in records in other tables: `sys_journal_field` for Journals, and `sc_item_option_m2m` for catalog variables.

a. To interact with catalog or record producer variables, access them directly, but append `.toString()` to ensure that you get a **primitive** and avoid pass-by-reference issues. (e.g. `current.variables.requested_for.toString();`)

3. **Dot-walking**

a. Using `.toString()` is also a good means of getting a **primitive** value from a **dot-walked** field (E.g. `current.request.short_description.toString()`). Just remember not to dot-walk through more than three layers. If you must dot-walk more than three layers, use the `.getRefRecord()` API of the server-side GlideElement object instead. If doing this client-side, be sure to use the GlideRecord `.getReference()` API with a callback function (more info in the "AJAX & Display Business Rules" section).

Pro-tip. Getting a journal field's value, like setting it, is different than you might expect. Neither `gr.getValue('work_notes')`, *nor* `gr.work_notes` *will likely give you the value you're looking for. Instead, call the* `.getJournalEntry()` *method of the* **GlideElement** *class like so:*

```
gr.work_notes.getJournalEntry(1);
//Returns only the most recent journal entry.
gr.work_notes.getJournalEntry(-1);
//Returns all journal entries, delimited by "\n\n"
```

Fig. 1.16: Two ways to get journal entries from a GlideRecord

The really important thing about using `.getValue()` specifically (the exceptions above notwithstanding), is to get a primitive value and avoid **pass-by-reference**, which can quickly weave a tangled web of references and unexpected behaviors. The `.getValue()` API is the best-practice way of doing this, but you can also use `gr.field_name.toString()`, as mentioned above.

You may occasionally be tempted to use `gr.field_name + ''` which relies on JavaScript's **implicit type-coercion** functionality, which is... fine... but there are issues, as JavaScript's type-coercion can behave unexpectedly, especially if you have a more complex statement. Further, since your server-side code is actually evaluated in **Mozilla Rhino** (a Java-based implementation of the JavaScript language), through a layer of Java (which does not have implicit type coercion), you may end up with a "serialized character array" rather than a proper String, which is... complicated... and bad.

The most efficient and best-practice-ey way to retrieve a primitive value, is nearly always to use `.getValue()`.

CONSISTENCY

It's important to be **consistent**, at least within any one script, because otherwise you risk making basic syntactic or grammatical errors *extremely difficult* to troubleshoot. You also risk being beaten about the cranium by the next developer who has to slog through your inconsistent code.

Consistency is important even when it comes to things beyond normal coding and naming conventions. A classic example of this sort of consistency (or lack thereof), is **string delimiters**.

Technically, JavaScript will handle any unique string declaration so long as the beginning and ending quote-marks match, and it will ignore any other string-delimiters. Rather, it won't "ignore" them, but it'll treat them as *part of the string* rather than as "control characters" that indicates the beginning or end of the string). For example, consider the following script (and be sure to read its contents):

```
var goodToKnow = 'Even though this string contains
"double-quotes", I don\'t have to escape them, ' +
'because the string began with a single-quote. \n' +
'I do, however, have to "escape" apostrophes, or the
interpreter will think I\'m ending my string. ' +
"If I wanted to switch to double-quotes mid-string, I
could (using the plus operator), and then I " +
"wouldn't have to escape the apostrophe/single-quote
anymore but would then have to escape double-quotes. " +
"But if I did that, I'd surely annoy whoever tried to
update my code later on!";
```
*Fig. 1.17: A very – **very** – annoying string[12].*

Personally, I – *your dashing and hilarious author* - use single-quotes (like `'this'`) as opposed to double-quotes (like `"this"`) almost all the time. This is because the double-quote takes an extra key-stroke (**SHIFT**), and **I'm extraordinarily lazy**...

Just kidding (...sort of...); it's because I declare strings more frequently than I use conjunctions within them, which would require escaping the apostrophes, as in the word `isn\'t`; so it makes sense for me. If you prefer to use **double-quotes** (`""`), that is also fine! Just make sure you're **consistent** within your

---

[12] *Just in case you have difficulty reading that string, it says:*

*Even though this string contains "double-quotes", I don't have to escape them, because the string began with a single-quote. I do, however, have to "escape" apostrophes, or the interpreter will think I'm ending my string. If I wanted to switch to double-quotes mid-string, I could (using the plus operator), and then I wouldn't have to escape the apostrophe/single-quote anymore but would then have to escape double-quotes. **But if I did that, I'd surely annoy whoever tried to update my code later on!***

scripts. The same goes for any other optional conventions. Whenever you have options, just be sure to be consistent!

The same rules about consistency apply to things like curly-brace placement. It's a pretty good idea to maintain consistency within your own code and, as much as possible, within the instance as a whole, when it comes to things like curly-brace placement. For example, the following code demonstrates a **non-standard** way of writing a conditional block:

```
if (recordIsValid){
    //do something with the record
}

else
{
    //throw an error message
}
```

Fig. 1.18: Ugly, annoying, terrible, inconsistent brace-style

This is a little more difficult to follow than it needs to be, because the curly-brace placement is **inconsistent**, and there is a white-space (line break) gap between the 'if' and 'else' blocks, which makes it much harder to follow and to know at a glance, that the two blocks are functionally connected.

Instead, here is the more commonly accepted "standard" way of writing a conditional block:

```
if (recordIsValid) {
    //do something with the record
} else {
    //throw an error message
}
```

Fig. 1.19: 1TBS; the one true brace style

This style of curly-brace placement is called "1TBS", which stands for "One True Brace Style". All the cool kids are using it.

To quote an article on brace styles[13] on 2ality.com:

> *"The de-facto standard in the JavaScript world is 1TBS, most style guides recommend it. One reason goes beyond taste and fitting in: If you return an object literal, you can't put the opening brace in a separate line. An object literal is not a code block, but things look more consistent and you are less likely to make mistakes if both are formatted the same way."[14]*

---

[13] *Yeah, I read articles about brace styles in my spare time. Why, what do **you** do? Have a **life**? Hah!*

[14] *This quote is from section "3: JavaScript" at the below URL:*

Finally, ensure that your **indentation** is consistent. The default ServiceNow IDE is not great at indentation, so be sure to click the "Format Code" ≡ button on the IDE, and visually scan through your code for indentation/spacing/line-break issues before saving it. Alternatively, you can just do what I do: Since the auto-formatter built into ServiceNow's browser-based IDE is frankly terrible and often wrong, I just write my code in an external IDE. I use WebStorm, but you can use VS Code, Notepad++, Sublime Text, or any of a great many other IDEs with built-in code formatting/"beautification" tools that you trust more than you do the browser-based one in ServiceNow's script editor fields.

FIELD SECURITY VS. FIELD OBSCURITY

It may be tempting to exclusively use UI Policies to control field visibility and mandatory state – they're just so convenient! - but whether you're talking about **UI Policies** or **Client Scripts**, it's important to realize that **any client-side-only measures** you take to make a field *hidden*, *mandatory*, or *read-only*, **can be thwarted** by a user with a browser! In fact, on rare occasions (such as if the user has a slow internet connection, or there is an error in an early loading client script), a field that's meant to be read-only may not appear that way right away when the page first loads, and could be edited without the user even intending to bypass any client-side protections you may have in place.

Hiding a field does not automatically clear its value! If you initially show a field, then conditionally hide it, but the user had entered a value whilst it was visible, that value will still be in the field, and it'll be saved to the database and potentially trigger logic too!

In more modern versions of the ServiceNow platform, there is now a checkbox on the UI Policy Actions that allows you to automatically clear the field value when the UI Policy Action runs, setting the field value to blank/empty, or "*—None –*" in the case of choice fields.

Any **client-side** measures to protect data, that aren't backed by a **server-side** component such as a *Business Rule, ACL,* or *Data Policy,* **can be bypassed**. Normally this is not a big deal. Some field protections are matters of convenience, or at least would not result in detrimental issues if the client-side field protections were ignored. However, in some cases (such as with approval records), field security can be extremely important.

Before committing to only using client-side field protection measures such as a *UI Policy* or *Client Script*, ask yourself what the impact would be if a user were to ignore those protections. If the impact would be significant, you should definitely consider an *ACL, Data Policy,* or possibly even a *Business Rule* to protect your data integrity instead.

CLIENT SCRIPTS & FIELD-LEVEL SECURITY

It's usually best not to use **Client Scripts** to control whether a field is *visible, mandatory,* or *read-only*; however, there are exceptions. For example, highly complex logic sometimes cannot be accommodated by one UI Policy. Complex multi-field conditions sometimes also cannot be accommodated. Occasionally, you might need to use a **Display Business Rule** to retrieve – for example – a system property value, store it to g_scratchpad[15], and use *that* to determine whether a field should be visible. These are all good reasons to use a Client Script to control whether a field is visible, mandatory, or read-only.

If you must use a Client Script instead of a UI Policy for some reason, be sure to document your reasons for doing so in your code or description, so other developers can understand why you did what you did, and don't waste time trying to "fix" it if there's a good reason for the approach you took. Also make sure that you have some logic in the client script that emulates what would be

---

[15] g_scratchpad is an object available in display Business Rules, which carries data from the server-side BR script, to the client-side g_scratchpad object for use in Client Scripts.
More on g_scratchpad in a later section.

the "**reverse if false**" functionality in a UI Policy (if the actions should be reversed if the condition is false), or at least provide some logic for how to behave when the condition is not (or is no longer) true. Be sure to also consider whether the logic should be applied when the form first loads (if `isLoading` is true), or if the triggering field of an *onChange* Client Script is blank (`newValue == ''`)

As a general rule, best practice dictates that if a UI Policy can do the job without an inordinate amount of fuss, use that over a Client Script; just because UI Policies are more clear, consistent, and easier to understand and update.

SETVISIBLE() VS. SETDISPLAY()

On the somewhat rare occasion that you need to hide a field using a **Client Script** (as opposed to a UI Policy), it is important to understand the difference between the `setVisible()` and `setDisplay()` methods of the `g_form` object in Client Scripts.

g_form.setVisible() hides the element inside the section, but leaves a **blank space** where the element was. I can imagine *some* situations where this might be desired, but the vast majority of the time, you'll want the entire section where the field or variable was, to **disappear** rather than leaving a blank space. In this case, you would use `g_form.setDisplay()`.

`.setVisible()` and `.setDisplay()` set the field's actual HTML document element's "visible" and "display" properties respectively, which is the reason for the difference in behavior; it relates to the difference in behavior of those field attributes.

See the screenshots below for examples.

Before running the script:

Requested for	Tim S. Woodruff	🔍	ⓘ
Location	United States	🔍	ⓘ
Due date	2018-02-01 10:50:28	📅	

Here's what that form section would look like, after running `g_form.setVisible('location', false);`:

Note the blank space where the field once was

Here is how that same form section would look after running the code `g_form.setDisplay('location', false);` instead of using `.setVisible()`:

Note that the field and the space it occupied are now both gone

*Note. While there **are** use-cases for hiding and showing fields using Client Scripts, such as when the conditions are too complex to be represented in a condition builder, I recommend that you default to using **UI Policies** and UI Policy Actions rather than Client Scripts to control field visibility (as well as whether a field is mandatory or read-only).*

BUSINESS RULE ORDER & .UPDATE()

One common point of confusion when dealing with scripts in Business Rules, is when to use `current.update()`. The answer to this question becomes intuitive, once you have a clear understanding of how the different types of Business Rules work. There are four ways a Business Rule can run, indicated by the **When** field on the form:

- Before
- After
- Async
- Display

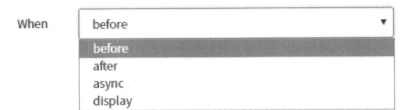

The **When** field on the Business Rule dictates several things about its behavior, and what parameters are available to scripts. First, recall that Business Rules are triggered by database options (*insert*, *update*, *delete*, or sometimes on *query*[16]). With this in mind, the values in the **When** field make a bit more sense.

Let's discuss each of the options for "when" a Business Rule runs, how they alter the behavior of our Business Rule, and what we can and can't do with each:

BEFORE

The **before** option means that the Business Rule will run **before** the *insert*, *update*, or *delete* operation is committed to the database. This means that you can still stop the operation by using `current.setAbortAction(true);`. This also means that you **do not** need to call the `current.update()` API in order to commit any changes that you make, because the record is already "on its way to the database", and will be committed after all "*before*" logic is finished running, assuming that the operation is not aborted by either using current.setAbortAction(true), or by executing a business rule with the "Abort action" checkbox checked.

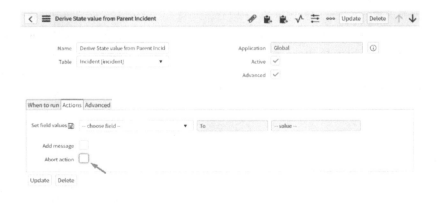

---

[16] *For more information on Query Business Rules and why they can be tricky and (if used incorrectly) even harmful, see my article on the subject on SN Pro Tips:* https://qbr.snc.guru.

Before Business Rules are useful for when you need to alter something about the record itself before it ever touches the database or prevent the database operation from happening at all. They should *not* (generally) be used to update **other** records – that is what *"after"* and *"async"* Business Rules are for.

To reiterate: **"before"** Business Rules are generally for **updating the record which triggered them to run**. You should *not* use a "before" Business Rule on the Requested Item [*sc_req_item*] table to create or update a Catalog Task [*sc_task*].

AFTER

The **after** option means that the Business Rule will run **after** the database operation, but *before* the user's browser is refreshed.

If you make a change to the record in an *"after"* Business Rule, it will **not** be committed to the database unless you call `current.update()`. However, if you need to update the current record in this way, it's almost always best to use a *"before"* Business Rule. It is *extremely rare* to have a good use-case for calling `current.update()` in any Business Rule. Making a change to the "`current`" record and then calling `current.update()` in an *"after"* Business Rule would actually re-trigger any business logic (including your *"after"* Business Rule), since it constitutes a *new* database operation. This could even lead to an infinite loop!

"So," you might be asking, "what, then, *are 'after'* Business Rules used for?"

Although they should not be used to update the `current` record, *"after"* Business Rules are fantastically useful for updating **related** records; especially records that might be shown in **related lists** on the record that triggered the Business Rule. For example, if you're on a Request Item [*sc_req_item*] (RITM) record, and you have a Business Rule that runs based off of an event in that table, but it updates one or more child Catalog Task [*sc_task*] records (which are shown in the related list at the bottom of the RITM record), then an **after** Business Rule is usually the way to go. However, if you need to update another type of record that *doesn't* need to be displayed when the form reloads after an update, an **async** rule is best.

Why? Because while *"before"* and *"after"* Business Rules are *running*, the user is *waiting*! These types of Business Rules run **synchronously**, meaning that the user has to sit around and wait for *entire milliseconds* while those operations finish running.

Async Business Rules, as we'll learn below, are different.

ASYNC

The **async** option in the **When** field, indicates that a business rule should run asynchronously, whenever the system scheduler is able to run it (usually within just a few seconds). This means that after saving a record, the server **does not wait** for async Business Rules to finish running before returning control to the user, and reloading the form (or whatever page the user will be directed to).

Async business rules are an extremely useful tool for maximizing performance and creating a positive and snappy user experience, but it is important to be aware of the side-effects of using Async over a different sort of Business Rule. For example, if you use an **async** Business Rule to update a record that will be displayed in a related list on the form that the user will see when the page refreshes, then when you load the form and view that related list, you will (usually) not see those changes. This is because when the related record was loaded from the database when the form reloads, it's likely that the async Business Rule would not yet have had a chance to run.

The up-side to **async** Business Rules, is that it is much more efficient and user-friendly to perform certain operations asynchronously (and therefore provide a much better user experience, when used correctly!) For example, updating a peripheral or related record which is **not** shown on the form, or triggering some other operation such as a REST API call to update or trigger some logic in some external system that doesn't need to be done *immediately* upon the triggering record being updated. If the operation can stand to wait a few seconds, make it async! The only exception here, is that the previous object (the state of the triggering record *before* the update that triggered the BR was made) is not available in async BRs, so if you *need* access to that, you might still need to use an "after" Business Rule to perform that operation.

DISPLAY

Finally, we come to **display** Business Rules. These are a little bit different than the other types we discussed above.

Display Business Rules run *after* the record is **retrieved** from the database. This means that they are not triggered by any changes to the record itself. Instead, they are triggered by the record being loaded from the database to be displayed in a form or interacted with in a script.

The results of these Business Rules can sometimes be a little bit unintuitive, since they modify data that's sent from the server, *without modifying the record itself* (unless you call current.update() in a *"display"* Business Rule, which... don't). This means that it's possible that you'd end up seeing data in the form which does not match the data in the database! For this reason, **display** Business Rules are not often used to modify any records. Instead, they're most commonly used to populate the **scratchpad**[17], which is an object that's used to make certain data available on the client; usually for client scripts. This is extremely useful from a performance perspective, so we go into detail about the scratchpad in the **AJAX & Display Business Rules** section!

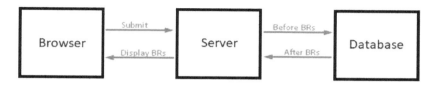

AJAX & DISPLAY BUSINESS RULES

There are a multitude of reasons you might need to communicate between the client, and the server (such as in a *Client Script*, *Catalog Client Script*, or *UI Policy*), including:

- Retrieving a **system property** to determine whether a field should be visible (*or for whatever reason you want, I'm not your dad*)
- Checking some value on another record in another table, possibly to determine how some logic on the front-end should behave
- Retrieving the GlideRecord object for a record being *referenced* on a form, to get the value in some field on that referenced record[18]
- Dealing with date/time objects, and calculating system time

With the notable exception of certain Client Scripts which must run on **submit**, it's always important to make sure we're performing **asynchronous** server requests in client-side code. In most cases, this can be done by specifying

---

[17] More info on the scratchpad, and how to use it with "display" Business Rules, in the "*AJAX & Display Business Rules*" section.

[18] It isn't possible to "dot-walk" using the `g_form` APIs in a Client Script, so you'll have to use something like `g_form.getReference()` (asynchronously) in the Client Script to retrieve a record before you can retrieve its field values. However, a common mistake is to use `g_form.getReference()` to get a GlideRecord object for a referenced record, in order to retrieve its sys_id. This is unnecessary, because the actual value of the reference field itself, is the referenced record's sys_id!

You can retrieve a referenced record's sys_id by simply using `g_form.getValue('some_reference_field');`.

Orlando API docs for the g_form.getReference() API can be found at:

https://developer.servicenow.com/dev.do#!/reference/api/orlando/client/c_GlideFormAPI#r_GlideFormGetReference_String_Function a **callback function** (such as when using the GlideRecord `.query()` method client-side), or by using **GlideAjax**.

Pro-tip: Need to perform a query in an onSubmit Client Script, but not able to run it synchronously (such as if your code needs to run on the Service Portal)? I've written a method for doing that, which you can see in my article: Asynchronous onSubmit Client Scripts:
http://onsubmit.snc.guru/

If you know **in advance** that you're going to need certain information nearly every time a given form is loaded, you can use a **display Business Rule** to grab the data from the server as the form loads, and pass it up to the client. Display Business Rules are a special type of script that run on the **server** when you request a record's data from the database, in order to load a form.

Pro-tip: It's not within the scope of this handbook, but if you're not sure how to make your request run asynchronously, I've written an entire article on the topic over at SN Pro Tips: http://ajax.snc.guru/

Once your browser requests the page and record from the database to display in the form, the display Business Rule runs **on the server** *if* the record you're loading matches the condition in the Business Rule. In that script, you could modify the data in the "current" object if you want to change how the record is shown in the form, but you'll also have access to the g_scratchpad object. You can **add properties** to this object in the *display Business Rule*, and these properties will be available to any *Client Script*, *UI Policy*, or *UI Action* running on that form via the same g_scratchpad object.

Note: This does not work for Catalog Client Scripts. You'll have to rely on asynchronous AJAX requests to the server in that case.

Display Business Rules are probably the most effective and **efficient** way of retrieving data from the server, but they are sometimes overkill. For example, if you only need the data that you would load into g_scratchpad in one special circumstance based on some rare client-side event, it might make sense to use a **GlideAjax** call instead. Just make sure that it's asynchronous!

GlideAjax is the second most efficient means of retrieving data from the server. However, unlike display Business Rules, GlideAjax typically requires both a client-side, *and* a server-side component, so it can be a bit more complicated.

Pro tip: If you look up the documentation on GlideAjax, you'll find that you can add "nodes" to the returned AJAX, which is useful for returning multiple or complex values from a single call. However, a much easier and cleaner way of doing this, is to return an **object** *populated with the values you need returned, in properties of that object. The object will then be available when you get the* 'answer' *node of the returned XML, and you can work with it directly. Much simpler!*

More details on this, GlideAjax, and asynchronicity in general, in my article at: *http://ajax.snc.guru/*

Finally, the *least* efficient method that's *still acceptable* in a pinch, is an **asynchronous** GlideRecord call. The same article linked above, will walk you through how to make a GlideRecord call happen asynchronously. You can also find documentation on all of these APIs in the ServiceNow developer site (https://developer.servicenow.com/), for specifics on how to use them.

To reiterate: If you know exactly what data you need to retrieve from the server in advance, and the conditions under which you want to retrieve the data are known on load, a **Display Business Rule** is probably the best option.

If that isn't the case, then **GlideAjax** is likely the best option.

For small, efficient queries (such as only returning one record in a script that runs only occasionally), an *asynchronous* **GlideRecord** query can be used.

For getting a GlideRecord object from a **reference** field, calling g_form.getReference() asynchronously with a **callback function** makes the query asynchronous, and is also acceptable (especially if you're only retrieving a single record).

DOM MANIPULATION

In the **Service Portal** (The "NOW" platform's fancy user-friendly front-end), DOM (Document Object Model) manipulation is almost entirely deprecated. There are ways around it, but ServiceNow officially recommends avoiding it at virtually all costs; not just in the Service Portal but, for future compatibility reasons, everywhere.

For this reason, it's important to use OOB methods whenever possible, that allow you to avoid DOM manipulation. The same applies to *synchronous* GlideRecord queries, and GlideAjax calls. Even in *onSubmit* Catalog Client Scripts. This means that we need to develop workarounds for certain bits of functionality which required either synchronicity, or DOM access. A great example of this, is requiring attachments on submission of a catalog item. There is virtually no easy way to do this without DOM manipulation, so you can't really do it in the Service Portal out of the box.

Note: *The best method that I've been able to come up with for validating attachments in the Service Portal, has a Script Include component, and a **JS Include**. These scripts create a new, custom API in the Service Portal:* `sp_form.getAttachments()`*. This API is not available out-of-box and must be implemented to work. You can find details on how to implement it at* http://portalattachments.snc.guru/.

For a Catalog Client Script to work in the Service Portal, it needs to be set to a type of either "All" or "Mobile / Service Portal". If the latter is selected, it will **only** work in the Service Portal.

Virtually all Catalog Client Scripts should have their **type** field set to **All**, but one exception is if you have one script to provide certain functionality in the "desktop"/classic view, and another corresponding script to enable that functionality using different APIs or a different method, in the Service Portal. If this is the case, be sure to document that in your code so other developers will know what's going on if they read it!

WHEN *NOT* TO CODE

Making your code effective and efficient is important, but it's also important to ask yourself a few questions **before** writing a custom script to solve a problem.

As we've discussed elsewhere in this guide, many of the custom scripted solutions that could be done via Client Scripts, can (and should) instead be done via UI Policies. While there are some situations where using a Client Script instead is just fine, UI Policies are usually the way to go, whenever possible.

The same logic applies to Business Rules: While a custom scripted solution (AKA: An **Advanced** Business Rule) is often necessary, you'll find you can actually use the **Actions** tab of the Business Rule form to accomplish many common, simple tasks, surprisingly often.

The above Business Rule sets the Incident's Description to the same value as the Short description, as long as Short description is populated, but Description is not.

For a simple task like this, there is no need for an "Advanced" (scripted) Business Rule.

For example, say you have a catalog task, and you want it to be assigned to the same user as the parent RITM. You could write a script to do that, or much more preferably, you could use Actions on a Business Rule like so:

An important thing to note here, is that we're setting a field **on the record** that triggered the Business Rule (what would be the `current` record in an advanced Business Rule script). If we were to instead try to use a Business Rule to **set a field *on* a dot-walked record**, we *would* need to use an "Advanced" (scripted) Business Rule. This is because we would need to ensure that the dot-walked record itself was saved back to the database after the change was made, using `.update()`,

On a related note: If you find yourself setting a field (especially a custom field) to *the same value as another field* in a referenced record via dot-walking, you should carefully consider whether the field you're setting *is actually necessary* on the table it's on. Very often, an actual database column that contains a value derived by dot-walking through a reference field on the same record, can be replaced with a **derived** field. For example, consider the **Catalog Task** [sc_task] table again. Imagine we wanted to display the **Short Description**

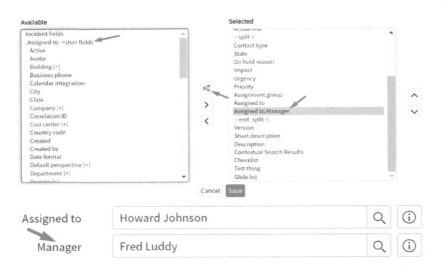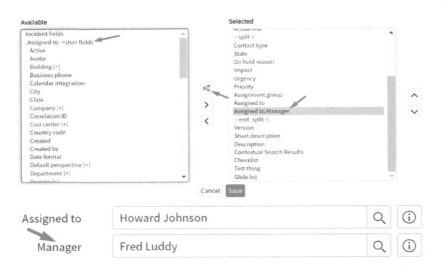

of the RITM, on the sc_task form. Well, we *could* create a new custom field called "RITM Short Description" [*u_ritm_short_description*], and automatically populate it using a client-side GlideAjax call, or a Business Rule's **Actions** tab, but if we did that, an architect might later come by and *hit us with a 101-key PS/2 IBM Model M buckling-spring keyboard.* Since those are very heavy, it would make far more sense to simply open the **Form Layout** tool, and add a derived field (AKA: a dot-walked field) that points to `request_item.short_description`. **This will show the derived field and its** value on the form.

Note that the "Manager" field can be easily edited on the Incident form, as it isn't read-only. This is usually not something that you'd want to leave as-is, because you don't want users to think they're just updating – for example - the Incident, when they'd actually be updating the **user's manager**. For this reason, it's wise to create a UI Policy that protects this dot-walked field on the form on which it's displayed.

*Note: Unfortunately, there has been a "bug" in ServiceNow for some time, that you cannot **set** a field on a record in another table by using dot-walking in the **Actions** tab of a Business Rule. You can **get** a value from a related record by dot-walking, but not set one. For that, you'll have to use a script.*

DEBUGGING

Why the thing is doing the thing

That's not a bug, it's a feature.[19]
—Microsoft

I think this guy might actually be a moron.
—My rubber duck

When troubleshooting the behavior of a client- or server-side script or object, remember to check the basics first. If you aren't sure what's causing some behavior, if feasible, start by disabling the object (Business Rule, Client Script, line of code, etc.) that you think is causing it, and see if that resolves it. If not, that object *probably* isn't the culprit. Additionally, don't forget to consider the other scripts that could be triggered if your script changes something in a form or field!

Business Rules might be running whenever you make a change, and that could be the true root of a given problem. Your Client Script could be altering a field, which triggers another onChange Client Script that runs on that field. Your Script Include could be invoking some external code that has other side-effects. A "query" Business Rule could be filtering your query unexpectedly, or even triggering strange and unintuitive behavior of certain types of SQL queries (which you can read more about in my article, at https://qbr.snc.guru).

Using the **debugging tools** built into ServiceNow is a great way to find out what's going on when you're not sure what script might be causing some behavior you're seeing. The debugging tools can be found in the Application Navigator, under **System Diagnostics > Session Debug**[20].

---

[19] *Translation: "I couldn't figure out how to fix that bug".*
[20] *Pro-tip: Debugging the Debugger*
Sometimes if you've been fiddling with the debugger window for a little while, it'll just stop "catching" breakpoints.

In this section, we're going to discuss some of the more effective, but often under-utilized methods of debugging **scripts**, both server-side, and client-side.

---

*The window may look like debugging is enabled, but it's not for some reason. If this happens to you, just **Pause** and then re-start debugging by pressing the Stop Debugging button (which looks like a pause icon), and then clicking the **Start Debugging** icon that replaces it.*

If that doesn't work, close and then reopen the debugger window.

SERVER-SIDE DEBUGGING

When it comes to debugging server-side behavior, you can add breakpoints to your code using the script editor, by clicking on the line number. For example, in the below screenshot, this Script Include has a breakpoint on *line 15*:

```
 1     var TimeZoneUtils = Class.create();
 2     TimeZoneUtils.prototype = {
 3
 4        /**
 5         * Upon initialization, you can pass in a GlideDateTime object you've already created and set to a specific
        time.
 6         * The reference to this object will be used, and your GDT will be modified in-place. Alternatively, you may
        choose
 7         * not to specify a parameter upon initialization, and a new GlideDateTime object will be created, used, and
        returned
 8         * with the current time in the specified time zone.
 9         *
10         * @param {GlideDateTime} [gdt] - A reference to the (optional) GlideDateTime object to be modified IN-PLACE.
11         * If not specified, a new one will be generated, and a reference returned.
12        */
13        initialize: function(gdt) {
14            if (gdt) {
15                this.gdt = gdt;
16            } else {
17                this.gdt = new GlideDateTime();
18            }
19        },
20
```

If you open the Script Debugger (**System Diagnostics > Script Debugger**), then all scripts with breakpoints you've created will show there. While debugging, any time those scripts are executed, the transaction will pause[21] and allow you to inspect variables in the local scope and see what might be causing any aberrant behavior.

Once you have the server-side script debugger window open and at least one breakpoint added into your script, trigger any synchronous server-side script you want to debug (such as by calling a Script Include method in **Scripts – Background** or by doing some action which triggers a Business Rule you're

---

[21] *If you notice that the debugger isn't pausing on your breakpoint and you've already tried stopping/starting the debugger, consider that certain lines of code may not actually be "executed" in the typical way that we think of code executing. That is, the JavaScript runner is made up of a bunch of different parts, each responsible for different jobs. The lexer and scoping engine for example, don't "execute code" in the way you might expect the actual JS "Engine" to. Only code executed by the Engine can be paused on. This means that if you do something like "hoist" a variable (which is a good idea much of the time!), and **declare** it without **initializing** it to a value, the JS Engine will not pause on the line in which you've declared the variable, even if you add a breakpoint there! I know this sounds a little arcane, but consider the following code:*

```
var myName;
myName = 'Tim';
var yourName = 'Bob';
```

Fig. 2.01

*A breakpoint on **lines 2 or 3** would pause execution just as you'd expect, but a breakpoint on **line 1** would not.*

trying to debug), and it should pause at your breakpoint. At that point, switch over to the debugger window and you should see something like this:

The line highlighted in red is the line we're currently paused on. The highlighted line has not yet executed; it's the line which *will* execute on the next "**step**" we tell the debugger to take.

If you look at the top-right of the above image, you'll see a section called **Local**, in which all of our locally defined variables are visible. This allows us to inspect current variable values as our code executes. Unfortunately, sometimes this doesn't work. Certain arrays and objects are shown as "Native JavaScript Array" or some arbitrary-sounding memory location address. As of the Paris release of ServiceNow though, we can get around this using the **Console** at the bottom of the debugger, which we'll discuss in more detail below.

Just above the **Local** section, you'll see five buttons that allow you to control the debugger, step through your code, and step into or out of function calls.

The function of these buttons may not be obvious when first glancing at their icons, so let's talk about what each of them does. Going in order from left to right, these are their functions:

1. **Stop Debugging**: This button, which looks like a pause icon, will stop the debugger entirely. Any code which is currently paused, will **resume**, and no further debugging will happen (even if your code hits another breakpoint) until you click the button again, to re-start the debugger.

2. **Resume Execution**: This button, which looks like a 'play' icon, will not halt debugging entirely, but will resume unmanaged execution of your code. Unlike the **Stop Debugging** button though, this button **will** pause execution at the *next* breakpoint it hits. For example, if you have a breakpoint *inside* a `while` loop, execution will pause the first time you loop through that code. You can "step" through the code from there and follow its execution, or you can just press the **Resume Execution** button, and your code will resume. However, the *next* time the loop runs, your code will pause again, and control will be given back to you via the debugger, just like the first time through.

3. **Step Over Next Function Call**: This is the button you're likely to click the most. It basically says, "execute the current highlighted line (highlighted in red) and pause execution on the next line". This is very similar to the **Step Into Next Function Call** button, except that it will stay at the current "layer" of the call-stack. This means that if the line to be executed is a function-call, unlike the "Step Into" button, this "Step Over" button will not step *into* the called function, and pause execution *inside* the called function, but will instead execute the called function in its entirety (without debugging *that* function line-by-line) and pause on the next line of the *current* function. Hence the name: Step *Over* rather than Step *Into*.

4. **Step Into Next Function Call**: As alluded to above, rather than staying at the current "layer" of the call stack, if possible, this button will step *into* the function being called on the highlighted line of code being debugged. If the highlighted line of code executes an outside Script Include, another method within an existing Script Include, or any other type of script that you have access to, the debugger will switch to that script, adding it to the **Call Stack** section in the panel on the left of the debugger window, and will allow you to debug execution of *that* script line-by-line, even if you didn't have a breakpoint in that called function. Note that I said, "any type of script *that you have access to*". There are some scripts you won't be able to step into; black-box code, such as any call to the ServiceNow GlideSystem API (for example, `gs.nowDateTime()`). In cases like this, pressing the **Step Into** button won't do any harm, and will simply behave as though you clicked the **Step Over** button.

5. **Step Out of Current Function**: This button is the exact opposite of the **Step Into** button. If you look at the **Call Stack** section in the panel on the left side of the debugger, you can see what scope is just "above" your current "layer" of the call stack. This makes it easy to **Step Into** a function call, have a look at how the first few lines are executing, then

easily return to the function you were debugging previously (the one which called this other function), by clicking the **Step Out** button.

The Script Debugger is an exceptionally useful, and largely under-utilized tool for exploring the behavior of your server-side code. I _**strongly**_ recommend becoming extremely familiar with this tool, its capabilities and limitations, and how to use it to effectively debug your own code during a rubber duck debugging[22] exercise.

**Pro-tip:** Only **synchronous** operations can be debugged since the debugger has to pause the thread as it executes in order to debug it. This means that certain things like inbound API calls cannot be debugged.

That said, for REST APIs in particular, you can trigger an API call using the Rest API Explorer (**System Web Services > REST > REST API Explorer**) to run it synchronously and debug your Scripted REST APIs (SRAPIs).

DEBUGGER CONSOLE

In addition to letting you see the exact values of all of your local variables, monitor execution line-by-line, step into and out of other functions, and generally become a wizard of debugging, the debugger has one more trick up its sleeve. As of the **Paris** release of ServiceNow, the debugger now has a **Console**.

You may have seen the Console section at the bottom of some of the screenshots in the previous section. Collapsed by default, it gives you just what you'd expect: a console into which you can write code. This can be monumentally useful for things like logging _actual_ values, including (a) variables which don't show up meaningfully in the **Local** panel at the top right of the debugger, and (b) values not stored in discrete variables, such as the value returned by `grIncident.getRowCount()`.

To get a value to print out in the console, you don't use `console.log()` like in a browser console, and you don't use `gs.info()` or `gs.log()` like in a background script. Instead, you simply type in some code, and whatever the last line of code[23] evaluates to, will be printed in the console. For example, if I'm debugging a Business Rule, and I simply type in the console

---

[22] _**"Rubber Ducking"**, also known as **"Rubber Duck Debugging"** is the practice of explaining, out loud, exactly what you expect your code to be doing, literally line-by-line, to an inanimate object, such as a rubber duck._

See rubberduckdebugging.com for more info.

[23] _If you write a line of code and press Enter in the debugger console, that line will execute. You can write multiple lines of code – even an entire self-executing function – by instead using SHIFT+Enter to create new lines, then pressing Enter when you're ready to execute the whole thing. Just remember that whatever the **last line of code evaluates to**, is what will be printed in the console._

`current.isNewRecord();`, **either** `true` **or** `false` **will be printed to the** console (depending on whether the Business Rule is executing on a new or existing record, obviously).

Example of running a line of code in the console, and the result being evaluated and logged below.

That's pretty rad, but the console can do much more than just log stuff for us. Consider the following screenshot:

This script is paused on line 14, and you can see that the variable `me` has already been declared and initialized, with the property `is_cool` set to `false`. Therefore, if we were to continue execution, we would see that the `else` block fires, as the condition in the `if` block is not met.

That is obviously unjust, untrue, and cruel beyond measure. Tim Woodruff is *way cool*! Therefore, as the debugger is paused on the line on which the condition in the if block is to be evaluated, we'll use the debugger to modify the value of `me.is_cool` so that it properly reflects Tim's totally tubular coolness.

As you can see from the screenshot above, in the **Local** panel at the top-right of the debugger, the `is_cool` property of the `me` object is now – justly[24] – set to `true`[25], and all is right with the world again.

But wait! Our code is still paused! The condition on line 14 has not yet been evaluated! Is it possible that the fiddling we did in the console will actually change how our code runs? **Indeed, it is!**

Of course, any changes you make through the console **only apply for this specific debugging instance,** and won't change how your code will execute in the future. However, this functionality does give you the ability to test out various changes **mid-execution,** *while* your code is running, and see how it behaves! That makes this one of the **most powerful tools in your entire debugging arsenal**!

If you've never taken the time to get familiar with it before, let today be the day! Go, now! Put this book down and go experiment with the Script Debugger!

No wait, come back, finish reading plz. :(

---

[24] *If you doubt the veracity of this statement, then allow me to present as evidence, the fact that Tim once wore mirrored sunglasses to class every day for like 3 months in middle school.*

Checkmate, chum.

[25] *If a variable's value is modified through the console, it won't actually immediately show the new value of the variable in the **Local** panel of the debugger until the panel is updated by, for example, stepping into the next line of code. However, you can also simply collapse and re-expand any object definition in the **Local** panel or the **Function** section in the **Closures** panel in order to see the updated values without having to step into the next line of code.*

CLIENT-SIDE DEBUGGING

When dealing with **synchronous, server-side scripts**, the ServiceNow Script Debugger makes debugging a breeze (most of the time), as you can actually see into the call stack and the contents of your server-side variables as you step through your code, line-by-line. When available, that tool is incredibly useful. Unfortunately, it does not work with client scripts.

So, how do you troubleshoot **client-side** scripts in ServiceNow, such as Client Scripts, UI Scripts, and Catalog Client Scripts? Well, since those scripts execute inside the user's browser, you're going to have to use some browser-magic to make that happen. The good news is, modern browsers already have an incredible debugger that's at least about as good as the server-side script debugger in ServiceNow, built right in!

*Pro-tip: Just like you can use "**Scripts – Background**" from the Application Navigator to run "background scripts" to execute arbitrary server-side code for testing purposes, you can do the same with client-side code by loading any record form and pressing CTRL+SHIFT+J to open the client-side script executor! This is a great tool for testing client-side code.*

The question then becomes: "How do I trigger the client-side debugger? I can't easily put breakpoints in my code that runs client-side, especially if it runs on-load; right?"

In fact, you can! Better yet, you can put calls to the debugger **directly in your code**! In this section, we're going to see exactly how to do that, using a not-very-smart Client Script that runs on the Incident form.

I find that the answer by way of example is usually most effective, so let's look at an example where we might need to troubleshoot a Client Script[26]: Let's say we work for a company whose *management* is all about the *micro*. They seem adamant that for some unknowable reason, they need to be added to the "watch list" on every single Incident that one of their direct reports is assigned to.

"Okay, sure" you say, as you die a little inside, and you go off to build this functionality for them.

From a previous 'enhancement', you've already got the "Manager" field on the form, which is auto populated whenever the `assigned_to` field changes. You reckon you can use that field.

---

[26] *I'm going to use a regular ol' **Client Script** here, but this simple method works with **Catalog Client Scripts**, client-side **UI Policy scripts**, **UI Scripts**, and even client-side scripts in the Service Portal! Basically, anything that executes as written, in the user's browser.*

You create a new Client Script on the Incident table, you have it run "**onChange**", and trigger it by changes to the "**Assigned to**" field. Then, you write a bit of code. This code does the following:

1. Gets the value of the "manager" field.
2. Gets the current value of the watch list, as an array (or a blank array if the watch list is empty).
3. If the manager field is blank, or the manager is already on the watch list, halt and do nothing.
4. Add the manager to the watch list array, then update the value of the watch list field.

All pretty straight-forward. Here's what that Client Script looks like once you're finished:

Name	Add manager to watch list		Application	Global
Table	Incident [incident] ▾		Active	✓
UI Type	All ⌄		Inherited	
Type	onChange ⌄		Global	✓
Field name	Assigned to ⌄			
Description	Helpdesk managers at this company are super micro-managey and lame, so they want to be added to the watch list whenever an agent is assigned to a ticket. This is a pretty shit example of a Client Script; this logic should probably actually be done server-side, because otherwise tickets created or updated outside the form view (such as via API) will not trigger this logic. This is just for demo purposes; don't replicate this lame functionality client-side. At least not without backing it up server-side.			
Messages				

Script 🖫 ⑦ ⅍ ▭ ▣ ▦ ▦ ⌕ ⌄ ⌃ ▣ ◎ 🖫 ⅍

```
 1   function onChange(control, oldValue, newValue, isLoading, isTemplate) {
 2       if (isLoading || newValue === '') {
 3           return;
 4       }
 5
 6       var assigneeMgrID = g_form.getValue('manager');
 7       var watchList = g_form.getValue('watch_list');
 8
 9       //If watch list has anything in it, split it into an array;
10       // otherwise, replace with a blank array.
11       watchList = (watchList ? watchList.split(',') : []);
12
13       //If manager is empty or already on watch list, halt and do nothing.
14       if (!assigneeMgrID || watchList.indexOf(assigneeMgrID) >= 0) {
15           return;
16       }
17
18       watchList.push(assigneeMgrID); //Add manager to watch list array
19       g_form.setValue('watch_list', watchList.join(',')); //update watch list field
20   }
```

However, when we trigger this code, nothing seems to actually happen! What's going wrong here?

We could add a bunch of log statements into our code and faff about with it until we figure out what the problem is, and then hopefully remember how to get our code back into the state we need it in and remove all of our debug log code... Or, we could add just one line of code, such as on line 8 in the below code:

```
function onChange(control, oldValue, newValue, isLoading,
isTemplate) {
   if (isLoading || newValue === '') {
       return;
   }

   var assigneeMgrID = g_form.getValue('manager');
   var watchList = g_form.getValue('watch_list');
   debugger;
   //If watch list has anything in it, split it into an
array;
   // otherwise, replace with a blank array.
   watchList = (watchList ? watchList.split(',') : []);

   //If manager is empty or already on watch list, halt
and do nothing.
```

```
   if (!assigneeMgrID || watchList.indexOf(assigneeMgrID)
>= 0) {
       return;
   }

   watchList.push(assigneeMgrID);
   //Add manager to watch list array
   g_form.setValue('watch_list', watchList.join(','));
   //update watch list field

}
```

Fig. 2.02: Adding the debugger statement to a Client Script

All we did here, was add a line with the statement `debugger;` on line 8, but now if we press **F12** to open the console and then re-trigger our code, we get something more like this (the Google Chrome debugger):

The Chrome JavaScript debugger

If you look closely, you may see some familiar elements, such as the **Resume Execution**, **Step Over**, **Step Into**, and **Step Out** buttons, a **Call Stack** panel, and a **Console**. These all behave pretty darn similarly to their counterparts in the ServiceNow server-side Script Debugger that we explored earlier in this chapter.

As you can see, the debugger has halted execution on the line in our code that has the `debugger;` statement. This can all look pretty overwhelming at first, but the main thing to pay attention to, is the **Scope** section. By default (in Chrome), this will be just below the **Call Stack** panel section on the right side of the debugger. Collapse Call Stack, and you'll see Scope. In the Scope section, **Local** is usually going to be the most relevant bit. That'll show you the values of the variables in your code at the moment the code halted, just like in the ServiceNow server-side Script Debugger!

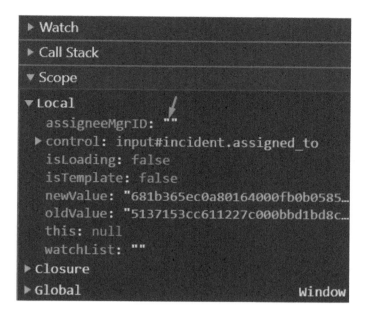

As you can see in the above image, the variables in the local function scope in my code look as you'd expect, except for `assigneeMgrID`. Since the code paused *after* that variable was assigned, we would expect that variable to have a value!

We can use the buttons at the top-right of the debugger to step line-by-line through my code, or even into or out of a given function-call, or we can use **Step Over** to remain at the current level of the call stack (meaning keep the debugger on our current code, rather than step into a function our code is calling).

By advancing step-by-step through my code, we can see that it's evaluating our `if` block's condition to be true, because `assigneeMgrID` is blank. This is causing the script to return early, and not do what we expected it to do.

Now that the debugger has helped us figure this out, we might go and investigate why this is. In this case, the issue is being caused by the fact that the Manager field is a dot-walked field (also known as a "derived field"). This means that unfortunately, my `g_form.getValue('manager')` line would not work, because the field "manager" doesn't actually exist on this record.

I could change that line to `g_form.getValue('assigned_to.manager')`, but that wouldn't work either because the Client Script triggers when the **Assigned to** field is changed, not when the dot-walked/derived **Manager** field is changed. (You can't trigger a client script on change of a dot-walked/derived field). The **Manager** field is updated **asynchronously** when the **Assigned to** field is updated, so when our logic runs, the *assigned_to.manager* field has not yet been populated.

In order to get this code to work, we'll need to do an asynchronous query of some sort to get the user's manager, but that highlights another benefit of the debugger; statement: you can even put it in your asynchronous/callback functions!

Pro-tip: If you need to debug a callback function, adding debugger; *in your asynchronous/callback function **will** halt execution, allowing you to debug it. However, your current state may be lost, and some related code won't be visible. You can work around this though, by simply adding a second debugger; line in the code that runs synchronously, and just pressing the **Continue Execution** (play) button in the console debugger UI when that debugger line in your synchronous code is hit. That will allow your callback function to be debugged effectively, without losing context!*

COMMON BUGS

There are some specific, common "bugs" that new and even mid-to-senior-level ServiceNow developers run into. In this section, we'll go over a few of them to look out for.

.UPDATE() IN BUSINESS RULES

In short: Never do this.

In *long: Almost* never do this.

While there is **no** reason to use **current**.update() in a Business Rule (**or in any code that's called from a Business Rule**), there are some occasions when it's appropriate to use the .update() GlideRecord API method. Just not on current. Virtually every such exception applies to **after** Business Rules (Business Rules configured to run **after** the database operation that triggered it has finished).

If the record which triggered the BR needs to be updated in some way, that update should happen in a **before** Business Rule (which runs on the application server *before* the updated record is sent to the database). "Before" BRs effectively intercept the data on its way to the database server, running their code at that point, and *then* sending the resultant record (including any modifications) to the database (unless something like `current.setAbortAction(true)` is used). Because of this fact, using current.update() in a *before* Business Rule is neither necessary, nor wise – the record you've updated is *already on its way to the database*.

If you need to update a **peripheral** record (not the record that's in the `current` object in the Business Rule, but perhaps a referenced or related record), then it is reasonable to do so using `.update()`; **however**, updating of peripheral records should be done in an **after** Business Rule; not **before**. In fact, if the records that need updating are not directly referenced on the current record (or otherwise don't require the change to take place *immediately*, those changes should be made in an **async** Business Rule, so that the user who submitted the form that triggered the Business Rule doesn't have to wait for the completion of that peripheral update!

The reason it's important to not use `current.update()` in a Business Rule, is that to do so would trigger a **second** update of the record; one for the transaction that triggered the BR in the first place, and a second one for the `current.update()` line in the BR's code. This could even lead to an **infinite loop**! The second update could trigger the Business Rule to run again, which would then trigger another update, which triggers the BR again, and so on, ad infinitum. Talk about *performance-hell*!

.UPDATE() CAN ALSO INSERT

There are multiple ways that you can end up with a GlideRecord object that doesn't contain a valid record. You could dot-walk into a broken or invalid reference field, fail to use an `if` block to validate that `.next()` or `.get()` returned a record from the database, or just forget to perform an actual query with your GlideRecord object in the first place.

In these cases, your code may continue executing, setting fields on the record and then attempt to update the record using `.update()`. It would not be crazy of you to think that `.update()` will *only update an existing record*, but in fact, `.update()` is something of a misnomer. Perhaps `.insertOrUpdate()` would've been a more accurate name for this method, since it will actually **insert** a record into the database if the GlideRecord object doesn't reference an existing record!

.SETWORKFLOW(FALSE) VS. .AUTOSYSFIELDS(FALSE)

You may have occasion to use `.setWorkflow(false)` to prevent Business Rules, Flows, Workflows, and other automated trigger logic from running as a result of some scripted record update. It is important to keep in mind that this will also prevent certain cascade operations from running, such as cascade deletes. This can result in negative side-effects, such as orphaned records or broken references. That said, there are plenty of perfectly legitimate use-cases for using `.setWorkflow(false)`.

What developers often forget to do when writing a script that updates a record that they don't want to result in any changes other than what they've written though, is to also use `.autoSysFields(false)`. This GlideRecord API method quite simply prevents the automatic system fields like `sys_created_on`, `sys_updated_on`, and `sys_updated_by`, from being updated due to your change. This can be a very useful API. Unlike `.setWorkflow(false)`, it actually works in a scoped app (though it doesn't accomplish the same goal). It's also useful for preventing a mass-update script from making – for example – every Incident in the Incident table appear to have been updated very recently, if you need to perform some small operation on all Incidents. That may mess up sort orders, reports, dashboards, and more; so don't forget to use `.autoSysFields(false)` when appropriate!

LIMITING QUERY RESULTS

One error that I see new and mid-level developers making **very** often, is to write a query that *seems* to expect only a single record, but not **enforcing** (or even **validating**) that fact. Consider the following code:

```
function getOpenTicketNumberByUser(userSysID) {
    var ticketNumber;
    var grTask = new GlideRecord('task');
    if (!userSysID) {
        throw new Error(
            'Invalid user sys_id passed in.'
        );
    }
    grTask.addActiveQuery();
    grTask.addQuery('opened_by', userSysID);
    grTask.query();
    while (grTask.next()) {
        ticketNumber = grTask.getValue('number');
    }
    return ticketNumber;
}
```

Fig. 2.03

This code has a few problems. First, it **assumes** that a given user would only have created a single open task (of any type). Because it's using a while loop on line 12, this code would actually loop through all of the user's open tickets and return the ticket number of the **last** ticket the query finds. Even if we switch this while to an if block though, we would still only return the **first** such ticket in the database.

In addition to being extremely inefficient[27], this code will almost certainly result in unexpected and unpredictable results.

This specific use-case is probably something that needs to be re-thought in general, but we can make some drastic improvements with just a few changes:

First, significantly refining the query to ensure that if we only expect one record, we actually do only *get* one record.

Adding .setLimit(1) (and changing the while to an if block) is also a good idea, to ensure that we do indeed only get one record, even if more records matching our query exist in the database. This would also drastically improve our performance since the query runner would stop "seeking" through the database after finding the first matching result. If there is only one match, this should improve query times by about 50% on average.

---

[27] *For more info on writing highly efficient queries, see the Performance chapter of this book.*

Another option might be to check whether our assumption (that there is only *one* matching record) is true, and log some error if not. That can be done in a relatively efficient way by using `.setLimit(2)`, `.hasNext()`, and switching the `while` to an `if` block, like so:

```
function getOpenTicketNumberByUser(userSysID) {
    var ticketNumber;
    var grTask = new GlideRecord('task');
    if (!userSysID) {
        throw new Error(
            'Invalid user sys_id passed in.'
        );
    }
    grTask.addActiveQuery();
    grTask.addQuery('opened_by', userSysID);
    grTask.setLimit(2);
    grTask.query();
    if (grTask.next()) {
        ticketNumber = grTask.getValue('number');
        if (grTask.hasNext()) {
            //In our system, users should
            // only have one open task!
            gs.error(
                'User with sys_id ' + userSysID +
                ' has more than one open ticket!'
            );
        }
    }
    return ticketNumber;
}
```

Fig. 2.04

In this updated code, I've highlighted the relevant changes in bold. As you can see, we're now using `.setLimit(2)`, an if block, and checking if a second record matching our query exists.

Note that **if there actually is only one open ticket** for this user, then using `.setLimit(2)` is no more efficient than not using `.setLimit()` at all. However, in the edge case that this code is detecting on lines 15-21 (a user having multiple open tickets at once), it will improve performance significantly.

Just a reminder though, as I mentioned earlier in this section, this is almost certainly a **bad pattern**. This assumes an environment in which users are actually *expected* to only have a single open ticket at a time – which is crazy.

NAMING CONVENTIONS

How to be kind to your future

self

There are only two hard things in Computer Science:
cache invalidation and naming things.
—Phil Karlton

What the heck does "inBusStNasS" mean!?
—Me, all the time

Whether it's a variable, a field, a parameter, a descriptor, a table, or anything else – names and labels matter! With the exception of variable names like `theValueForDeterminingIfARecordIsActive`, more descriptive field names are generally preferred. Imagine if that variable were instead called `FldValActvDet`. Without context, you'd have a heck of a time figuring out what sort of data it might contain! This isn't a tweet or a T9 SMS from 1993, so don't be afraid to use vowels and complete words in your variable names.

The most important thing about naming conventions, is that they **make sense**. If you're not certain about what to do, or not confident of the best solution, ask your team! Your company or client might have an existing standard around naming conventions; and if not, creating one is a great way to show initiative! Taking a little responsibility for maintaining the quality of your instance is a great way to build a name for yourself within your organization and get a career boost because of it!

TABLES

One of the most commonly neglected conventions around table naming, is to always give your table a **singular** name. **Fields** can have plural names if they can hold multiple values, but tables should always have a singular name. This applies to both the **name**, and the **label** of a table.

Consider some of the core ITIL tables: *incident, sc_cat_item, problem*, and *change*. These tables all have singular names. They are not named "incidents", or "problems", for example. In the table's dictionary record, there will be a place to enter the pluralized version of the table label, which can be used to describe multiple records in that table. The system will default to the table's label followed by an "s". However, if you have a table labeled something like **Logbook Entry** [u_logbook_entry], the system might pluralize it as **Logbook Entrys**, which is not the correct spelling. In this case, you would have to update the plural label to **Logbook Entries**, but the label would remain singular.

__Note:__ The latest versions of ServiceNow seems to do a little better with correctly pluralizing most words in table names for the pluralized labels but be sure to double-check!

There are a few OOB table names that defy this rule, but that doesn't mean that we should emulate this mistake! For example, the **System Properties** [sys_properties] table is pluralized. This is a remnant of very old versions of ServiceNow, and since table names are very difficult to change without major system-wide impacts, it has remained plural.

Another good general rule for table naming conventions, is to follow a separate convention when naming certain specialized types of tables. For example, **data lookup** tables are tables which define the relationship between selections in certain fields in a given record, in order to facilitate some business logic. A data lookup table might therefore contain a set of fields and corresponding values that, when found on a **task** record, should result in assignment to a specific group, or the record being set to a specific priority. When creating a data lookup table, it's not a bad idea to begin the table name with **u_dl**. You can create new Data Lookup Definitions from the **System Policy > Rules > Data Lookup Definitions** module in the Application Navigator.

*__Note:__ In order to automatically apply certain business logic, your custom data lookup table must extend the **Data Lookup Matcher Rules** [dl_matcher] table. You may need to enable the **Data Lookup and Record Matching Support** table to enable this.*

Similarly, **many-to-many** tables should usually have a name beginning with **u_m2m**. These naming conventions are less *friendly* than for normal tables, but they help to make it clear when you're working with tables that serve a specific utilitarian function. For example, **dl_matcher_incident_priority** makes it clear that we're dealing with a utility table, whereas a name like **incident_priority** would be much less clear (Is this a list of Incident priorities?)

As for case: table **labels** should always be in **"Title Case"** (with the first letter of each word being capitalized) Of course, acronyms can be fully capitalized.

FIELD NAMES AND LABELS

In general, names should reflect labels and vice-versa. If you have a field labeled **Business justification**, it should not be named "u_string_3", nor "u_ncc_ad_string", nor even the less-unacceptable "u_bus_jus". Unless the label needs to be quite long for some reason (in which case you might want to reach out to other team members or an architect for advice), it usually makes sense to have the name match. In this case: **u_business_justification**.

Also remember that it's not necessary to include the table name in your field labels or names. For example, the **Number** field on the Incident table is not named **incident_number**, or labeled **Incident number**. It's just **Number**. This is because it's clear that it's the Incident number, given that it's on the Incident table. If it were a reference to a different table, a name indicating the table it references might be more appropriate. For example, a field on the Incident table which references the Problem table might appropriately be called **Related problem** with the name **u_related_problem**. However, if it's a field that might need to be changed to reference a different or more "base" table in the future, you might leave the **name** (which is difficult to change) vague (like **u_related_task**), but have the **label** be **Related problem**.

In the same vein, it is usually unnecessary to add "ID" or "number" (as just a couple of examples) to a field name or label. For example, if you have a field which references the Incident table, where the display value is the **Number** field, you do not need to name the field **Incident number**, or **Incident ID**. Simply **Incident** is sufficient for a label and is recommended. It will contain the number as the display value, sure, but it'll also contain a reference to the entire record which allows you to view all of the other details as well. In a sense, the field wouldn't contain the Incident number, it would contain the entire Incident (or at least, a reference to the entire Incident).

Although **table labels** should be in **"Title Case"**, **field labels** should be in **"Sentence case"** (with only the first word being capitalized). This rule probably has more exceptions than most, but since table and field dictionary records are both stored in the same table, this case-convention is a good idea. Of course, acronyms can be in all-caps no matter where they appear in the label.

Finally, **Catalog variables** are not the same as database columns, and so do not use the same naming standards. For catalog variables, the **Question** field determines what should be shown on the form. This can be a question (such as "What is the business justification?" or a leading statement (such as "Business justification"). However, the **Name** field on a catalog variable definition uses a more formal standard. It should contain no spaces, and – like database column names – should be *snake_case*. Unlike custom database columns though, you do *not* need to precede catalog variable names with "u_".

VARIABLES

*Note: This section only refers to **JavaScript** variables, not **catalog** variables.*

JavaScript variables that point to **functions**, **objects**, and **primitives** should be in **camelCase**. **Class** names on the other hand, should be in **TitleCase**. All variable names should start with a letter (a lower-case letter, in the case of non-class variables). Finally, Constants should be in all-uppercase. For example:

```
var MYCUSTOMTABLEQUERY =
'u_active=true^sys_updated_onONLast
30days@javascript:gs.beginningOfLast30Days()@javascript:gs
.endOfLast30Days()';
```
Fig. 3.01

Note: JS doesn't technically have "classes" per se, but we implement them on the ServiceNow server-side using Script Includes. So for those, we use TitleCase.

The following example script contains multiple examples of various variable types, and best-practice naming conventions for them.

```
var assigneeSysID = getAssigneeSysID('Johnny B
Developer');

function getAssigneeSysID(assigneeName) {
    var assigneeUtils;
    gs.debug('Got argument: "' + arg + '".',
'exampleArgument');
    var grUser = new GlideRecord('sys_user');
    //If user is found
```

```
if (grUser.get('name', assigneeName)) {
    assigneeUtils = new AssigneeUtils();
//Check if the user is a valid assignee. If so, return
the user's sys_id.
    //Otherwise, fall out of conditional blocks
        if (assigneeUtils.checkIfValidAssignee(grUser)) {
            return grUser.getUniqueValue();
        }
    }
//If user cannot be found, or the user is not a
// valid assignee, fall through to return false

    return false;
}
```

Fig. 3.02

Another good rule of thumb when it comes to variable declaration, is to never declare variables inside of loop initializations (like `while` or `for` loops). This would lead to them being re-initialized on every loop! It's also not a good idea because if that loop never fires, then the variable is never initialized; so, if it were used outside of the loop, it would be undefined and may result in an error. Also, if you had a **nested** loop that used the same iterator, you would get very surprising behavior indeed; possibly even resulting in an infinite loop.

It's also not a good idea to declare a variable inside a conditional or loop code-block (`if`/`while`/`for`) like so:

```
var i = 12;
while (i < 10) {
    var howMany = i + 42;
    i++;
}
console.log(howMany); //undefined!
```

Fig. 3.03

This is for several reasons, not least of which is that if the loop or conditional block doesn't run for some reason, accessing it outside of that block could result in an error that could be exposed to the user if un-caught. Instead, declare your variables just above your control and conditional blocks, or maybe even hoist the declaration all the way to the top of the function/scope.

When you initialize a variable, also consider initializing it to a **default** value. For example, integer variables might be initialized to -1 as a default value (unless it might end up being a negative number as part of normal operation) like so:

```
var i = 12;
var howMany = 0;
```

```
while (i < 10) {
    howMany = i + 42; //Dumb example, but go with it
    i++;
}

console.log(howMany);
```

Fig. 3.04

OBJECT PROPERTIES

Object **property names** (also called **Keys**) may contain underscores in lieu of spaces, or they may be declared in camelCase. The important thing is to make sure that your conventions are **consistent**, at least within any one set of functionality, as you can see below.

```
var myObj = {
    property_one: 'This is the first property',
    property_two: 42
};
myObj.property_three = 'This is the third property of
myObj';
myObj['property_four'] = true;
```

Fig. 3.05

GLIDERECORDS

My preference is that GlideRecord variables should begin with gr, but some people prefer to end their GlideRecord variable names with GR instead, or do something totally different. Either way, GlideRecord variables should usually indicate the table name, or at least something about the record that is identifiable.

GlideRecord variables should also be singular; not plural. It might be tempting to call your variable something like grReqItems, but remember that at any given time, that variable only contains a **single record**, and should therefore be singular. **Arrays** however, are often plural. For example:

```
var sectionNames = g_form.getSectionNames();
```

It's alright to just name your GlideRecord variable after the table name (grIncident, for example). However, it's also acceptable (and often wise) to indicate something about the **query**. For example, you might name your GlideRecord variable grOpenIncident to indicate that you're iterating through only Incident records where the **Active** field is set to true. Just remember that if you modify your code and change the query or something else about the variable and need to change its name to match, you should update its name **scope-wide**, so that the variable name always corresponds to its contents. This is *especially* important when you have multiple GlideRecords on a single table.

Even if you don't have multiple GlideRecords on a single table, it's a good idea to name your GlideRecord variables with more descriptive names. Just remember to keep them singular in most cases.

```
var grOpenIncident = new GlideRecord('incident');
grOpenIncident.addActiveQuery(); //Get only open Incidents
grOpenIncident.query();
//etc...
```

Fig. 3.06

Pro-tip: *It's a good idea, for Glide objects at least, to indicate type in the variable name. For example, similar to GlideRecord variables beginning with "gr", a GlideDateTime object might begin with "gdt" as in* var gdtNoonYesterday = new GlideDateTime();.

ITERATORS

Iterators are similar to normal variables, except that they store some information which relates to the state of the loop in which they're used, and should be used in block-scope only. This means that if you have a for() {} block, the iterator variable you use should typically only be used inside the curly braces that define the code block that executes for each iteration of that loop.

If you know what sort of things you're iterating through, it's a good idea to use a meaningful name, as you can see in the following example:

```
function Instance(name, url, production) {
    this.name = name;
    this.url = url;
    this.production = production;
}
var myInstances = {
    'dev': new Instance('dev', 'http://sndev.service-
now.com/', false),
    'test': new Instance('test', 'http://sntest.service-
now.com/', false),
    'prod': new Instance('prod', 'http://sn.service-
now.com/', true)
};
```

```
var snInstance;
for (snInstance in myInstances) {
    if (myInstances.hasOwnProperty(snInstance) &&
myInstances[snInstance].production === true) {
        console.log('The production instance URL is: ' +
myInstances[snInstance].url);
    }
}
```

Fig. 3.07

In the example above, I knew that I was iterating over an object consisting of ServiceNow **instances**, so I named my iterator variable snInstance. However, it's perfectly alright to use something like prop or even p as an iterator, as you can see here:

```
function Person(firstName, ageInYears, heightInCm, gender)
{
    this.firstName = firstName;
    this.ageInYears = ageInYears;
}
function Family(lastName, parents, children) {
    this.lastName = lastName;
    this.parents = parents;
    this.children = children;
}

var homerSimpson = new Person('Homer', 42);
var margeSimpson = new Person('Marge', 41);
var lisaSimpson = new Person('Lisa', 8);
var bartSimpton = new Person('Bart', 7);
var maggieSimpson = new Person('Maggie', 1);

var theSimpsons = new Family(
    'Simpson',
    [homerSimpson, margeSimpson], //parents
    [lisaSimpson, bartSimpton, maggieSimpson] //children
);

for (var p in theSimpsons) {
    if (theSimpsons.hasOwnProperty(p)) {
        console.log('This property is a(n) ' + typeof
theSimpsons[p]);
    }
}
```

Fig. 3.08

In the preceding snippet, we're iterating over the theSimpsons object, which contains a string, and two arrays. Each array then contains multiple Person objects. One very important thing to remember about iterators, is that if you have a **nested** loop, you should not use the same iterator name for the nested loop, as you did for the outer loop; otherwise the nested loop will override the value of the outer loop's iterator and could result in an infinite loop!

It is a good idea to avoid doing much heavy-lifting in a nested loop whenever possible. For example, it's not often a good idea to iterate over a GlideRecord inside a while loop that's already iterating over *another* GlideRecord. This would result in a separate query for every result in the outer loop! There is usually a better and more efficient way to do this, such as using the first query to populate an array of sys_ids, which can then be used in the query filter for the second lookup. Only use a nested query if you can't come up with a better solution.

When iterating over arrays, you always know that your iterator variable will contain an integer, since arrays do not contain named properties like other types of objects. In this case, as with the p iterator for object properties, it's perfectly alright to use an iterator with a name like i. You may also choose to use something more descriptive, like index or count. If you know that your array should contain only a specific type of thing, you may even choose to use a more appropriate name as you can see in the following example:

```
var food;
var favoriteFoods = [
    'non-dairy beef',
    'evaporated water',
    'raw halibut',
    'banana and pickle sandwiches'
];
var msg = 'I like...';
for (food = 0; food < favoriteFoods.length; food++) {
    if (food > 0) {
        msg += ' and '
    }
    msg += favoriteFoods[food];
}
console.log(msg + '!');
```
Fig. 3.09

However, the following notation would also have been completely acceptable for the loop above:

```
var i;
var favoriteFoods = [
    'non-dairy beef',
    'evaporated water',
    'raw halibut',
```

```
    'banana and pickle sandwiches'
];
for (i = 0; i < favoriteFoods.length; i++) {
    if (i > 0) {
        msg += ' and '
    }
    msg += favoriteFoods[i];
}
```

Fig. 3.10

In JavaScript, there are multiple ways to perform a loop in your code. When iterating over the properties of an object, it is common to use syntax similar to the following:

```
var prop;
for (prop in obj) {
    /*code here*/
}
```

Fig. 3.11

This is fine for a start, but remember that when you iterate over the properties of an object, you don't want to iterate over **non-enumerable** properties: properties along the inheritance chain, which can result in irretrievable values and undefined or inaccessible property names. To avoid that, whenever iterating over an object, the first line in that loop should be to check if the object indeed has the property you've stepped into, using the Object prototype's .hasOwnProperty() method, like so:

```
function Instance(name, url, production) {
    this.name = name;
    this.url = url;
    this.production = production;
}
var myInstances = {
    'dev': new Instance('dev', 'http://sndev.service-
now.com/', false),
    'test': new Instance('test', 'http://sntest.service-
now.com/', false),
    'prod': new Instance('prod', 'http://sn.service-
now.com/', true)
};
var snInstance;
for (snInstance in myInstances) {
    if (myInstances.hasOwnProperty(snInstance) &&
myInstances[snInstance].production === true) {
        console.log('The production instance URL is: ' +
myInstances[snInstance].url);
    }
}
```

Fig. 3.12

Note that the `myInstances` object consists of several other objects, generated from the `Instance` constructor/prototype. More information on constructors can be found in the **Constructors** section of this guide.

DATABASE VIEWS

It's a good idea to precede all database view names with "dv", and let the rest of the name be an indication of what tables are joined. As an example, joining the **Incident** table with the **Problem** table (for whatever reason you might do that) would result in a database view called something like **dv_incident_problem**.

This is just a technique for making it a little easier on yourself later if you ever have to look at a list of objects including tables and database views, to differentiate one from the other.

DUPLICATE VARIABLES

There are *rare* circumstances where it is appropriate to have a variable (either a JS variable or a catalog variable) with a number in it. However, it is almost always best to avoid having multiple fields of the same type, with the same name, and the same purpose, such as **u_name_1** and **u_name_2**. It is understood that this is occasionally unavoidable, but if a better solution can possibly be found, that is preferable. This applies to both **names** and **labels**. The same goes for database fields as well, and also applies to both label and name.

TABLES & COLUMNS

How not to ruin everything forever

A perfect database column is a rare thing. You could spend your whole life looking for one, and it would not be a wasted life.
—*Ken Watanabe, almost*

There are a lot of rules around tables and columns in ServiceNow, as in any relational database. These rules are important, since it can be very difficult (if not impossible) to change certain things about a table or field once it's created. Most of the rules will become more obvious, the more you understand about databases in general and ServiceNow in particular; however, this chapter has some general guidelines and specific advice to consider.

For table naming conventions, see the ***Naming Conventions > Tables*** section.

CUSTOM FIELDS

Creating custom fields is often necessary, but doing so can have serious performance implications if you're not careful, especially (*though not solely*) if it's done on the **Task** table or some other heavily extended base table. As such, you should ask yourself a few questions before adding any new database columns (AKA fields):

Is this field necessary?

Ask yourself: Does the data you expect this field to contain actually add value in some way? What does it add? Is there a better way to add that same value, or data?

Does this data already exist somewhere else?

As we'll discuss in the **Knowing When Not to Code** section of this document, it's important to have a sense of where your data is coming from, and where else it might exist. If it already exists elsewhere, it might make sense to grab the data from there using a **reference** or **calculated** field, or even a **derived** field. If it already exists on a referenced record, it almost always makes sense to use a derived field rather than a new, custom field.

If the field should always contain a scripted or calculated value, consider using the **Calculated** check-box on the field's dictionary record, scripting the calculated value there, and setting the field to read-only on the client. Also be aware that, just like using a Business Rule, calculated field scripts only run server-side.

For more information on calculated and default field values, see the ***Tables & Columns > Default vs. calculated field values*** *section.*

Should this field appear on the form, or list?

Once you create a new field, you need to decide if it'll be shown on the form or list. Make sure you're conscious of whether or not it's on the **default** form/list view, or any **specific** views other than Default.

What <u>label</u> and <u>name</u> should I give this field?

See the ***Field names and labels*** *sub-section of* ***the Naming Conventions*** *chapter of this guide for info on this.*

Who should be able to see or write to this field?

If the field should not be written to, it should be made **read-only**. If it must be written to, it should be made mandatory.

If it is more than trivially important that a field be made **mandatory** or **read-only**, a server-side component such as an **ACL**, **Data Policy**, or possibly a Business Rule with `current.setAbortAction(true)` in conjunction with a **UI Policy** should be used in order to enforce that logic server-side as well as client-side. If it is important that some users not see the field or its value at all, then an ACL should be used. This is because any client-side measures taken to secure a field from being viewed or edited can be overridden by a sufficiently mischievous user!

Pro-tip: If you decide to abort an operation by using `setAbortAction()`*, you should consider adding a condition check that the source of the action is an actual logged-in user session and not an API call or automated business logic, by using* `gs.getSession().isInteractive()`*. This is great for when you want to block a user from performing an operation, but you probably don't want to interfere with back-end processes that may need to save the record.*

REFERENCE FIELDS

Reference fields (or in database parlance: "Foreign Key (FK) fields") are a major component of most tables in ServiceNow. However, when a reference field "references" a very large table, the "auto-complete" and search functionality for records to reference in that field, can take a very long time as it queries the entire table.

One solution to this, is to pre-filter the list of available options for your reference field. This can be done using a **Reference Qualifier** on the field in question.

Using the same principles we'll discuss in the **Performance > Query Efficiency** section of this compendium, we can optimize the client-side performance of our reference field by limiting the number of possible results to be searched, for whatever string the user enters into the reference field. This makes the field much more responsive on the form.

EXTENDING TABLES

It's important to be careful and mindful about extending tables. If you only need one or two fields from a given table, you probably don't need to extend it. If there are only a few fields you *don't* need on the other hand, you probably *should* extend it!

Keep this in mind: if table **B** extends table **A**, you will see all of the records from table **B** *as well as* all the records from table **A**, when you view table **A**. This is because tables which extend other tables, sort of exist "inside" those tables, with the extension just containing a sort of *delta*, or a list of the differences between the extended table, and the extending table.

For an example of this, navigate directly to the **Task** [task] table and you'll see Incidents, Change records, and Problem records among others. This is because each of those tables extends the base **Task** [task] table!

THE TASK TABLE

The **Task** [task] table in ServiceNow's **"Now"** platform is an important base table which is extended by many others. It must be handled carefully, and protected. It is important to understand that on the back-end database, the **Task** table is actually one giant, flat table. (This can change in some configurations, but this is the typical database architecture.) Because of that fact, it is important to protect the table, avoid adding unnecessary fields to it, avoid making changes on the base table itself, and generally be careful and make sure we know what we're doing when we interact with it directly.

Avoid adding long string or other fields with unnecessarily large max lengths; especially to the **Task** [task] table, or tables which extend Task. This is because large fields obviously have a more significant impact on database operations and performance than smaller fields (even if not filled out to capacity).

Avoid creating new fields directly on the Task table, unless you're certain that you want it to be added to **every single table** which extends task. This holds true for modifying things like **labels** and **choice values** as well – unless you mean to have your change applied to all task tables (**Incident, Problem, Change,** etc.), don't make your changes on the base Task table. This is what **overrides** are for! Label overrides and dictionary overrides allow you to modify a field on just one task-based table, as opposed to on all. The same applies to any other table which extends another.

THE STATE FIELD

The **Task** table contains a field called **State** [state], which is so important that it warrants its own section. State is an **Integer** field, meaning that despite the string of text shown in the drop-down box (the field's **display value**), the actual field – both on the client, and on the server – contains an integer.

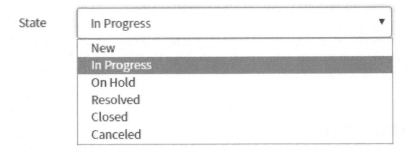

For this reason, and since it tends to drive the progress of a given ticket, we cannot go hacking away at the values and labels of this field. On Task-based tables in particular, there is a great deal of business logic that depends on the values in this field.

When creating new State field values, make sure that the values are numerically similar to other, similar values. For example, the OOB **"closed"** and **"cancelled"** states both have values equal to or greater than **7**. If I were to add a new state in which an Incident were no longer open, such as **"Abandoned"**, I might give it a value of **9** or **10** (as **"cancelled"** has a value of **8**).

The ServiceNow "Now" platform has some built-in logic that makes a few assumptions which are important to know about when dealing with the State field:

- Any option **value** that is equal to or greater than **7** is assumed to be **inactive**.
- Any option value that is **less than** 7, is assumed to be an **active** state.

If you want to add a new "inactive" State value (meaning that the ticket should be deactivated when it's in that state) such as **Abandoned**, you should set that state's **value** to a number equal to or greater than **7** (as long as it doesn't collide with any other State value).

By the same token, if you want to add a new **active** State value (one in which the ticket's **Active** field should remain **true**), you should use a value **less than** 7. Does this mean that you can only have 6 possible **Active** State field values? Not at all! If you run out of positive numbers that are less than 7, you can simply use **negative** numbers (-**1**, -**2**, etc.).

Nowadays, there isn't a lot of logic that's hard-coded to a particular State value; however, it's still a good idea to stick with the logic that if the value is >=**7**, it's an **inactive** state, and if it's <**7**, it's an **active** state due to legacy state-handling code. The "new" method that the platform uses to determine if a state should be "closed" (deactivated) or not, is based on the State field's **close_states** dictionary attribute, which the OOB Script Include **TaskStateUtil** uses. This dictionary attribute contains a **semicolon-delimited** list of the "closed" Task states.

Also notice the **default_close_state** dictionary attribute in the above screenshot, which is also used by the **TaskStateUtil** script.

Be careful not to confuse the **Value** of a given choice option, with the **Sequence** field. The Sequence field determines the order in which the options show up in the drop-down list.

When creating a new state model for a new table, consider also creating a helper **Script Include** to keep track of the state model for you. Consider the following example:

```
var MyTaskStates = Class.create();
MyTaskStates.prototype = {
    initialize: function() {
        this.DRAFT = -1;
```

```
    this.NEW = 1;
    this.WORK_IN_PROGRESS = 2;
    this.ON_HOLD = 3;
    this.PENDING = 4;
    this.COMPLETE = 7;
    this.CANCELLED = 8;
  },

  type: 'MyTaskStates'
};
```

Fig. 4.01

This is similar to the OOB Script Includes **IncidentState** and **IncidentStateSNC** (though implemented differently/more simply). You can access this state model like so:

```
var currentState = parseInt(current.getValue('state'));
if (currentState === new MyTaskStates().ON_HOLD ||
    currentState === new MyTaskStates().PENDING) {
  //do something when task is on hold
}
```

Fig. 4.02

It would be simple enough to create a **GlideAjax** (client-callable) version of this script as well, and that version could simply access the values in this version, so you only have to maintain one script. Or you could use a Display Business Rule that runs on every record in your custom Task-based table and pass the state model to the client using g_scratchpad.

DATABASE VIEWS

There are some best-practice guidelines for creating database views that we haven't yet discussed. If you are building a reporting application or working on an application which produces a dataset that may be used for reporting, you may consider using a **Database View** to present multiple tables' data coalesced together. For example, if you have an **Orders** table with a String field **User ID** that contains the User ID of the user for whom the order is placed, you may want to create a database view to "join" the Users table, and the Orders table together, so that you can report on any field on either table as though the data from both were all in one place. However, there is very often a better way.

In the example above, we should first of all be using a **Reference** field that points to the **Users** table, not a String field that contains a user's **User ID**. Once we've done that, we can simply **dot-walk** into the Users table, to grab the fields we want without using a Database View. For example, we can add a column to our report on the orders table that points to `ordered_for.department` to find the department of the user who ordered the thing, even though the department field is on the Users table, and we're reporting on the Orders table.

There are, however, some circumstances under which you must use a database view (or where it makes the most sense to use one). In these situations, there are still some additional guidelines:

- The "first" or **left** table should always be the table which we would expect to be smaller (to contain fewer records), as this makes it less database-intensive to generate the Database View.
- **Coalescing** should only be done on fields which have **database indexes**. You can find this in the table definition's related lists.
- Ensure that your table names and short-hands do not use any **SQL reserved words**. A list of reserved words can be found here: https://dev.mysql.com/doc/refman/5.7/en/keywords.html
- Non-admins do not have access to new Database Views by default, even if they would've had access to all constituent tables. Specific **ACLs** will need to be created for database views.
- Database Views can be particularly computationally intensive and are often not the best solution to a given problem. As such, it's a good idea to check with your team and/or your project's architect(s) before implementing any solutions involving a Database View prior to beginning development on it.

DEFAULT VS. CALCULATED FIELDS

It's common for new developers to think that giving a table column (or **field**) a **default** value, and giving it a **calculated** value, have effectively the same result. However, this is not the case. Default and calculated values behave quite differently, and should be used for quite different purposes. In this section, we'll explore what each is (and is not) used for, and the difference in behavior between them.

DEFAULT VALUES

Default field values can be quite simple: a string, an integer, or whatever data-type matches the field's type.

Default value	This is the default value!

You can get a fair bit more advanced with it though, by using the `javascript:` keyword in the beginning of your value. Any code after the `javascript:` is executed on the server when the form loads, or when a record is inserted into the database (but not when **updated**) without a value in that field.

Default value scripts will have access to the server-side `current` object, but remember that on a **new record** form, the default value is calculated on the server, before/while the form is loaded. At that time, there is no data in the `current` object.

If there is no value in the field when it is inserted into the database, then the default value will be applied. However, if **any** data exists in the field when the record is created, the default value is not calculated or used.

In addition to on insert (as long as the field is still blank when the record is saved), the default value is also calculated when the "new record" form is loaded, in order to be displayed in the "new record" form. With that in mind, consider the following code:

```
javascript:'Record created by ' +
gs.getUser().getDisplayName() + ' on ' +
current.getValue('sys_created_on') + '.';
```
Fig. 4.03

By using the `current` object in the above code, when the form loads, we're getting a **blank** value, but the rest of our code still executes. Thus, on the new record form, we'll see a default value like this:

```
Record created by John Smith on .
```

Note the lack of the expected creation date in the string. If we were to **erase** this value on the new record form or leave it blank by creating the record in a way that doesn't use the form (such as via a script or through **list editing**), then the default value would be re-evaluated on insert, at which point there would be a `current` object for it to reference, so we **would** get the expected output in that case. However, if we load the form, get the value with the missing creation date, and then save it, then the incorrect value will be saved to the database. The default value would not be re-evaluated on insert, because the field now has a value in it!

When creating a new record from the form, the default value will be pre-populated in the field to which it applied (as we learned above). However, you can prevent this from happening so that the default value only puts data into the field on **insert** (and not on the new record form) by checking if the current object is populated. Here is an example using the same code as above, but wrapped in a **conditional** block that should cause it to only populate the default value if the record is being inserted into the database (when the current object is available):

```
javascript:if (!current.sys_created_on.nil()) { 'This
record was created by ' + gs.getUser().getDisplayName() +
' on ' + current.getValue('sys_created_on'); }
```
Fig. 4.04

This behavior is what fundamentally separates the Default value functionality from the Calculated field functionality.

CALCULATED FIELDS

While **default** values apply only on form load or on insert, and are not re-evaluated if the field is updated later or if the value changes, **calculated** fields always apply, and are re-evaluated whenever the record is updated. Also, while a field's default value may be scripted using the javascript: keyword, calculated fields are **always** scripted.

*Note: Calculated fields are calculated **every time a row is read**. This means any calculation that does complex processing is re-run on every row read. In an example with 100 rows, that means a calculated field, even one which isn't displayed on your list, is calculated once per row or 100 times per list. **Often** you can get the **same results, and better performance** by using an Insert/Update Business Rule to set a field value, rather than relying on a calculated field. You should only use a calculated field if you have a good use-case for needing to update a field every time the record is read from the database.*

To enable setting a field as calculated, begin by loading the **Advanced** view of the field dictionary record, go to the **Calculated Value** form section, and check the **Calculated** box. This will enable the field calculation script editor:

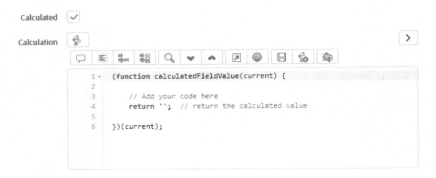

Calculated field values do have access to the `current` object (just like default value scripts), but since they are re-evaluated whenever the record is updated, it's less of an issue that the `current` object is empty when loading the **new record** form. Still though, to avoid a user seeing "*null*" in a calculated field on the new record form, it's often a good idea to put in some filler text to be displayed if the `current` object is empty, or even return a blank string in that case as you can see in the following script:

```
(function calculatedFieldValue(current) {

    var userName, updatedDate;
    if (current.sys_created_on.nil()) {
        return '';
    }
    var grUser = new GlideRecord('sys_user');
    if (grUser.get(gs.getUserID())) {
        userName = grUser.getDisplayValue();
        updatedDate = current.getValue('sys_updated_on');
        return 'Record updated by ' + userName + ' on ' +
updatedDate + '.';
    }
}) (current);
```

Fig. 4.05

LIST & FORM DESIGN

Guidelines for making happy

users

There are three responses to a piece of design – yes,
no, and WOW! Wow is the one to aim for.
—Milton Glaser

Know thy users.
—Socrates, if he'd been a developer

User Interface and Form design standards in ServiceNow include standards and designs for lists, forms, Catalog Items, and general guidelines for building intuitive, attractive, and informative interfaces. It's easy to forget to update the default list and form views when building a new table, or modifying an existing one, but to do so would cause a negative experience for the users of that table; especially if they aren't well-versed in the functionality available to them in ServiceNow, such as the ability to personalize their own list view.

In this chapter, we're going to learn about form and list design, layout best-practices, and how to make our interfaces intuitive. We'll learn about how the default layouts tend to "train" users to expect certain things, such as important at-a-glance information, to be in specific locations on a form, and how to leverage that to make navigating the interfaces we design, a breeze for our users.

FORM LAYOUTS

Form layouts may seem obvious, but it's often wise to take a moment to plan out how you want your forms to look and consider some of the design guidelines that the default form views seem to adhere to. As with the rest of this document, these are **general guidelines**; not hardline rules. Form design in particular, should be more about providing a positive, functional user experience, than about sticking to black-and-white rules. If you look at a form, and it just feels *off* somehow, it probably is.

If you're creating a new table, it means you're creating a new form as well. If you're adding a field to an existing table, that might often require a form update – and it is *rarely* wise to just drop the new field at the bottom (or top) of the form. Here are some general guidelines:

Most forms that need to display enough data to warrant it, are organized into three main sections:

1. A data-dense two-column section at the top, with critical "at-a-glance" details. Fields like **Number, Assigned to**, and **Priority** usually belong at the top.
2. The middle section of a form (if the form is long enough to warrant multiple sections), is often devoted to **additional data, multi-column fields**, and other info that's good to have on the form, but not required to know at a glance.
   a. If your form has more than three sections, consider adding the additional groups as **form sections** in the middle group.
   b. Remember that the form sections may display as **tabs** depending on the user's preferences. For this reason, it's important to make sure that related fields are shown in the same section, so users don't have to flip back-and-forth between tabs to see related data.
3. The last section is usually devoted to long **text** and **journal input** fields, with any **journal lists** at the very bottom of the form.
   a. You wouldn't want to have an **Activity log** in the middle of your form, because it can become quite long as activities are performed on the record; this could require a great deal of scrolling to see the rest of the fields. For this reason, the **activity** formatter should typically be one of the last elements on a form, before the related lists.
   b. Keep in mind that not all users have the **tabbed** form interface enabled, which means that if your activity section is not the last section on the form, some users will need to do a lot of

scrolling, even if it's in a separate section with other journal fields. This is usually not good.

It's rarely a good idea to put journal input fields anywhere except directly above **journal lists**; otherwise they may be mistaken for string fields, which can be very confusing.

While it doesn't have to be perfect, it's a good idea to try to design forms that are mostly **symmetrical**. This means that when using the **two-column** layout for a given section, you shouldn't put many more fields in one column than the other. Just be aware that if you have several fields in one column but only show one of them based on conditions on the form, then the form may look unbalanced in the **form designer**, but in a real-world scenario, the actual form may actually be balanced.

Ensure that you don't have the same field in two different places on the same form. Each field should only appear once on each view of the form (if at all).

If you need to modify the form for an OOB (Out-Of-Box) "admin-only" record, such as the ACL form (for example, to add a field that is not visible), be sure that it isn't captured in an **Update Set** – unless of course, you *want* it to be captured in an Update Set and propagated through the instance lifecycle! Just be mindful of whether you have an Update Set selected, and which Update Set it is. In fact, using Update Sets mindfully is probably good advice for nearly **everything** you might do in ServiceNow. It's the best way to keep your work on different projects in separate silos and keep your instances in sync.

LIST LAYOUTS

When creating a new table, it can be easy to forget to set up the **default** list view, but this is a crucial step! If users are going to see records in your table's list, you want to provide them with as much information as is reasonable, without overcrowding the list view on a reasonably sized browser window.

Often, a unique identifying field (though *not* sys_id) should be shown **first** in the list. An example of such a field, is the **Number** field on Task-derived tables. Following that, it's usually a good idea to include other important fields that a user would likely need to see at a glance. Fields like **Assigned to** on Task-based tables, for example. Finally, date fields are frequently placed on the far-right, but this is by no means a requirement. The important thing is not to clutter your list view with too many fields, or include long, non-wrapped text fields that would not display enough information in the list view to be useful.

Pro-tip. In order to make a String field appear as a larger multi-line input box on the form, set its **Max length** dictionary attribute to 256 or more characters, and it will appear as a large input field automatically. String fields with fewer than 256 maximum characters will show as single-line text input fields.

OOB RECORDS

Thinking "out of the box"

If it ain't yours, don't mess with it!
—My dad

Seriously, knock it off!
—My dad, again

Stop taking apart the neighbor's toys!!
—Still my dad

You **may occasionally run into situations** where you're tempted to either modify or replace an out-of-box record in ServiceNow, but it's important to keep a few guidelines in mind. In this chapter, we'll briefly discuss a few guidelines to consider.

For scripts in particular: **Do not modify OOB records if you can help it**! If it is an option, you may add a **condition** so the script does not run on your table, or in the circumstance you don't want it to. Then you can use **Insert and Stay** to duplicate the record, and configure it to run under the opposite condition (so it only runs when you **do** want it to).

This is important, because it's extremely difficult to know everything that might interface with, trigger, or utilize code in each script record. Modifying how it runs might very well trigger cascading bugs that will be extremely difficult to troubleshoot down the line. Also, when the instance is **upgraded** or **patched**, if one of the OOB records needs to be upgraded as part of that process, it cannot do so if the OOB record has been modified.

Of course, whenever you perform an upgrade, you should always **review skipped updates** (updates that were not deployed by the upgrade process because of customized out-of-box records). When we review the "skips", we'll see that only the condition has been changed, so we can keep the OOB record as-is, or merge it with any updates in the OOB script field (which will be easy, because we did not modify the script field). This protects your custom functionality, *and* the out-of-box functionality.

Another option for that used to be popular for replacing an OOB script's functionality, is to **deactivate** it, then create a copy of it with a different name and similar (but modified) functionality. You would have to be very careful to watch for bugs that arise from this though, if something unexpectedly tries to make use of or relies upon the old record. For that reason, this approach has fallen out of favor and is generally no longer recommended.

*__Pro-tip:__ It's a good idea to periodically check the system **warning** and **error** logs after each significant change to the system, and to monitor the logs in production from time to time. This will tell you if anything is misbehaving. By monitoring the logs closely and looking for the first instance of specific errors, you can often track down the Update Set that contained the change that caused the issue. This is also why it's a good idea to catch and log any potential errors you can predict in your code!*

EXTENDING OOB SCRIPT INCLUDES

For Script Includes, you can "*modify*" an OOB (or any other) Script Include, by **extending** it. Actually, extending a Script Include doesn't *actually* modify it, which is good! Instead, it involves creating a **new** Script Include that inherits the methods and properties of the one you're extending. From there, you can add new methods or properties to your Script Include, or you can override methods that were inherited from the one you're extending. It's *somewhat* rare that you should need to do this, but it's useful to understand how it is possible, so you don't have to modify an important OOB Script Include or re-implement a lot of functionality in an extant Script Include.

For an example of how this works, let's say you have the following Script Include in your instance already:

```
var ExampleScriptInclude = Class.create();
ExampleScriptInclude.prototype = {
    initialize: function() {
    },

    overrideMe: function() {
        return 'Override me!';
    },

    dontOverrideMeBro: function() {
        return this.overrideMsg;
    },

    overrideMsg: 'Don\'t override me, bro!',

    type: 'ExampleScriptInclude'
};
```

Fig. 6.01

If you'd like to override or add to it, you can do so by creating a **new** Script Include, and setting the prototype to `Object.extendsObject(ExampleScriptInclude, {});`, and adding any extensions or overrides into the object in the second argument like so:

```
var ExampleExtendedScript = Class.create();
ExampleExtendedScript.prototype =
Object.extendsObject(ExampleScriptInclude, {

    overrideMe: function() {
        return 'Thanks for overriding me!';
    },
```

```
    overrideMsg: 'Thanks for not overriding me!',

    type: 'ExampleExtendedScript'
});
```
Fig. 6.02

Here, we've **extended** the `ExampleScriptInclude` class in our
`ExampleExtendedScript` Script Include. We've **overridden** the
`overrideMe()` method (function) of that Script Include, by including a method
with the **same name** in our overriding Script Include. We also override the
`overrideMsg` variable, which is only used in the `dontOverrideMeBro()`
method of the `ExampleScriptInclude` class!

Even though `dontOverrideMeBro()` is not in `ExampleExtendedScript`,
it is still available to instances of the `ExampleExtendedScript` class because
it extends (and therefore inherits the properties and methods) of
`ExampleScriptInclude`. The same goes for the `overrideMsg` variable. So,
when we call `dontOverrideMeBro()`, it uses the overridden `overrideMsg`
property, and prints out the new message.

With the above two Script Includes in your instance, consider what would be
output from the following code:

```
var msg = '';
var parent = new ExampleScriptInclude();
var child = new ExampleExtendedScript();

msg += '\n==Parent Script==\n' +
    'Let\'s override this: \n\t' + parent.overrideMe() +
'\n' +
    'Don\'t override this: \n\t' +
parent.dontOverrideMeBro() + '\n';

msg += '\n==Extended/Child Script==\n' +
    'Now that it\'s overridden: \n\t' + child.overrideMe()
+ '\n' +
    'This method wasn\'t overridden, but the property it
uses was: \n\t' + child.dontOverrideMeBro() + '\n';

gs.print(msg);
```
Fig. 6.03

The results that would be printed out, look like this:

```
==Parent Script==
Let's override this:
Override me!
Don't override this:
```

```
Don't override me, bro!

==Extended/Child Script==
Now that it's overridden:
Thanks for overriding me!
This method wasn't overridden, but the property it uses
was:
Thanks for not overriding me!
```

Hopefully this effectively illustrates how overrides work, and how you can extend and override OOB Script Includes, *rather* than replace or modify them. It is typically okay to extend custom (non-OOB) Script Includes in-place, but it's not usually a good idea to modify any script's methods/properties in-place, if they're already being used elsewhere.

One last thing to consider about "OOB records" is that just because it's been done in the past – even if an OOB script does something a certain way, for example – it doesn't mean it's acceptable **now**. Things change, including best-practice standards, and even the underpinning architecture of the platform. For example, the change from **ES3** to **ES5** syntax support on the server, which changed how we handle lots of scripts ranging from JSON parsing and stringification, to how we interact with Arrays natively. If you don't know what the best practices are around a given technology, ask your team.

Pro-tip: If you're still not sure, you can also ask me! Get in touch any time via Twitter at @TheTimWoodruff

TESTING

The art of not looking like a dolt

*Pay attention to zeros. If there is a zero, someone
will divide by it.*
—Cem Kaner

*Before software can be reusable, it has first to be
usable.*
—Ralph Johnson

TESTING **is arguably** one of the most important parts of the software
development process, but it can also be one of the most tedious. It is
important though, as you might be surprised how often even veteran
developers find defects in their code or workflow. Finding bugs doesn't make
you a poor developer – it makes you a good one! Failing to *check* for bugs, is
what makes a poor developer.

In this chapter, we'll learn about *how* to test our code, as well as how to both
prevent errors, and catch them when they occur. We'll also learn about how to
use logs *correctly* and *efficiently*, without cluttering or spamming our system logs
with unnecessary information.

Note: *This chapter does not teach how to use the ServiceNow Automated Testing
Framework (ATF). It focuses more on the smoke-testing and functionality testing that
you should be doing,* **even if** *you also use the ATF!*

TESTING EXECUTION PATHS

It's important to **always test your execution paths**. An execution path is a logical "route" that a given bit of code could take, based on the **control flow** in the code. Control flow consists of any code which is evaluated to determine the path of execution your code goes down. if/else blocks are probably the most ubiquitous examples of control flow.

If you're writing a script, it almost goes without saying that you should give it a quick test to make sure it's working before moving on. However, what if your code has **multiple execution paths**? That is, what if your code does one thing in one set of circumstances, and another thing in another set of circumstances?

In that case, it's important (and wise) to test **each path of execution** that your code could take (each condition in the flow-control of your code).

Consider the following code:

```
if (g_form.getValue('state') === 3) {
    /* Do a thing */
} else if (g_form.getValue('state') === 4) {
    /* Do something different */
} else {
    /* Do yet a third thing */
}
```

Fig. 7.01

After saving the above Client Script, I might test it by first setting the value of the **state** field to 3, and making sure the appropriate code ran without errors, then setting it to 4 and checking, then setting it to something that's neither, and validating that the code in the else block also fires correctly. I would watch my testing browser's **console** for any errors that seemed related to my code, or – if I were writing server-side code – I would watch the **system logs**. Doing **anything less than this**, risks non-functional code getting into production, and making you look very silly indeed.

*Note: Don't forget to test an execution path that your code should **not** execute under as well! You wouldn't want to spend all that time verifying that your code works in all the circumstances you expect it to, only to find after releasing it into production, that it also executes when you **don't** want it to!*

Finally, don't forget to test each UI-type in which your code *might* run. For example, in the **Service Portal** chapter of this compendium, we'll learn about how the portal behaves differently and has a different subset of APIs than the rest of the platform. As such, if you build a catalog item, you should surely test it in the portal. However, even if your company typically does not use the "old CMS UI", there are occasions where you might automatically load a catalog item in that UI as an end-user. Therefore, it's often a good idea to test your catalog item (as well as any accompanying catalog client scripts or catalog UI policies) in the portal, **and** in the CMS UI.

I've got a simple tool that you can use to make it easier to quickly load a catalog item in a service portal on my blog, **SN Pro-Tips**: http://tryinportal.snc.guru/.

IMPERSONATION

It may be tempting to take the perspective *"I'm a developer, not a QA tester!"*, but if your work comes back from testing, it takes more time overall and more effort on your part. Plus, it doesn't look great having your work fail testing in ways that you should've caught yourself before marking it as done.

Simply taking the extra step of impersonating a user who you know should have the relevant permissions will go a long way to ensuring that your work doesn't fail testing, but it's also a good idea – if applicable – to test as a user that should **not** be able to see or do whatever it is you've built.

To that end, it's not a bad idea to request a **"Testing user"** when building out the requirements for a project, so you'll have one or more specific user accounts that you can use to test with, which you know should have access to the functionality in question (or *not* have access, in certain cases). A testing user is not necessarily or typically a new user account to be created for the project, but is instead a specific example user – a real person within the business – who *should* or *should not* have access to whatever functionality you're building, such as tables or front-end pages. You can impersonate that user account and attempt to access the resources in question; make sure that they can see the correct number of records, and all relevant columns, through whatever interfaces such a user might make use of.

Pro-tip: *Open an "Incognito" or "Private" browser tab and log into your ServiceNow instance there. In that tab, you can impersonate the testing user without impacting your other browser session.*

ERRORS

An important part of the testing process is looking for errors. Not just errors in functionality (though those are obviously also important to identify), but errors in your code. Even if your code *seems* to behave correctly, you may still have some code that throws errors; and you won't always know about them if you aren't looking for them!

While running your tests, it's a good idea to open your browser's **console** window and watch for any errors or warnings that show up. You can usually open the console by pressing **F12**. Any time your code performs any server-side operations, it's also a good idea to check the system error logs from **System Logs > System Log > Errors**.

To prevent hard errors in your code, and to handle *anticipated unexpected* situations, consider using a `try{}catch(){}` block. For example, if you expect a specific method to be present on some object, you may be pretty confident that it's there, but you can **anticipate** the *unexpected* scenario in which it's `undefined` by putting your code in a `try{}` block, and using the `catch(){}` block to "handle" the error by logging a specific message to the console (using `console.error()`) or system error logs (using `gs.logError()`, or the scoped `gs.error()`). The up-side of handling errors in this way, is that when you've **caught** an error, you can determine what to do after that. For example, consider the following code:

```
try {
    var priorityElement = gel("incident.priority");
    setPriorityBackgroundColor(priorityElement);
} catch(ex) {
    console.warn('Unable to get priority element or set
element color. Using alternative handling');
    alternateIndicatePriority(); //optional
}
```

Fig. 7.02

The above code attempts to use the `gel()` API to get the Incident priority field element. However, this API is not always available (and in general, should not be used in ServiceNow if it can be avoided, because it directly accesses the DOM). If this API is undefined, this would throw an error. By capturing that error in a `try{}` block, we can determine how to handle the error ourselves. The code in the `catch(){}` block will only fire in the event that the code in the `try{}` block throws an error. This allows us to use some alternative functionality for when `gel()` isn't available.

That said, if you **know** that your code may run where a certain API is unavailable, or if you know that your code otherwise might run into an error, it is preferable to **prevent** the error rather than **catch** it. For example, if this were a Catalog Client Script which we expected to at least occasionally be run in the Service Portal (where the `gel()` API is not available), we might rewrite this code as follows:

```
if (typeof gel !== 'undefined') {
    try {
        var priorityElement = gel("incident.priority");
        setPriorityBackgroundColor(priorityElement);
    } catch(ex) {
        console.warn('Unable to get priority element or
set element color. Using alternative handling');
        alternateIndicatePriority('some message');
//optional
    }
} else {
    alternateIndicatePriority('some other message');
}
```

Fig. 7.03

Above, we're still using the try/catch because developing **defensive** code is usually a good idea. However, we're doing so inside a condition which should **prevent** the `catch{}` block from being triggered most of the time, even if the `gel()` API is unavailable.

LOGGING

There are several logging APIs available to your scripts: Server-side, you've got `gs.log()`, `gs.debug()`, `gs.warn()`, `gs.logWarning()`, `gs.error()`, and `gs.logError()`. Client-side, you've got `jslog()`, `console.log()`, `console.warn()`, and `console.error()`.

Client-side, your logs will always show up in one of two places: In the browser console (which you can typically access by pressing **F12** on your keyboard with the browser window selected), or the "JavaScript Log". The JS Log can be shown by clicking on the **System Settings** cog in the top-right of the ServiceNow frame, and toggling the **JavaScript Log and Field Watcher** switch on.

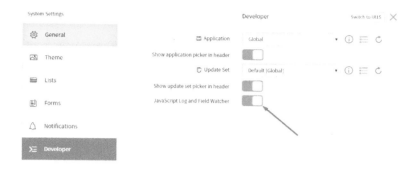

Once enabled, the JavaScript log will display at the bottom of each page, next to the **Field Watcher** (which helpfully displays information about what happens to a specific field and the causes for each change, after you right-click the field and choose "Watch – '[field]'").

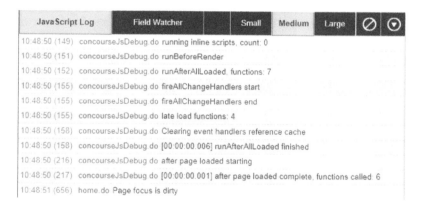

The rest of this section will refer primarily to server-side APIs, but whether server-side or client-side, there are a few important things to think about, when logging messages within your scripts:

- Will anyone ever need to know what you're logging?
- Does this log message contain sensitive data?
- Does this need to be logged *every time*, or just while debugging?
- If someone else sees your log message, are they going to be able to find the script that triggered it?
- Did you remove your "test" debug/log statements before deploying?

Let's address these questions one-by-one:

Will anyone ever need to know what you're logging?

This may go without saying, but if you're logging something, you should be sure that it's something that you might conceivably need to look up at some point. Don't log just for funzies; make sure there's a purpose behind it. There actually **is** a performance cost to a large number of unnecessary logs in an instance, and it adds up.

If you're logging something during development or debugging (for example, if you want to see whether your code is actually stepping into a conditional block so you add a log statement inside that block) that's fine, but be sure to remove those log statements before moving to production (as mentioned below).

Does this log message contain sensitive data?

This should also go without saying, but **never log passwords or other sensitive data**. **Ever**. Logs are not a remotely secure way to store data, and are only minimally ephemeral. Do not log sensitive data, or the values of fields which may contain sensitive data.

If you're dealing with passwords or something sensitive like that, you may log peripheral data related to it. For example, if you want to know whether you got a valid password value or not, consider checking that the length of the string is greater than some number of characters, or some other check which does not reveal the password itself, or anything which could make brute-forcing the password easier (For example, **do not** log the exact length, or first few digits of the password).

Do we need to log this *every time* your script runs?

When adding a log statement (assuming it's not just for testing and wouldn't be removed before deploying your code), consider whether you really need to log this message every single time the script runs. Whether it's a debug message, a warning, or an error message, consider wrapping it in a condition to determine if the log is necessary. You might also use a `try{}catch(){}` block, and only log if the `catch()` fires. Just don't spit out state-data to the log unless it's in some sort of "exception" state.

Would someone else be able to identify the source of the log?

There are some important differences between `gs.warn()` / `gs.error()`, and `gs.logWarning()` / `gs.logError()`. - `logWarning()` and `logError()` are not available in scoped apps, but they accept a second argument: the **source** of the log message. For example, consider the following code:

```
try {
    doSomething()
} catch(ex) {
    gs.logWarning('Handled exception: ' + ex.message,
'MyScriptInclude.thisMethod');
}
```

Fig. 7.04

The preceding code logs a **warning** to the system logs. The second argument after the log message itself, is the **source** of the warning message. In this case, it's the specific script include and method name in which the log message itself resides. This will allow someone who might see this warning in the future, to track down and troubleshoot the reasons for the warning.

While both `gs.logError()` and `gs.logWarning()` accept this second "source" argument, neither of these methods are available in scoped applications. The `gs.error()` and `gs.warn()` methods (which are available in-scope) do not treat additional arguments the same way. Instead, additional arguments to these methods will be used for string-replacement. For example...

```
gs.warn(
    'The ticket {0} is assigned to {1}, which is bad for
some reason.',
    current.getValue('number'),
    current.assigned_to.getDisplayValue()
);
```

Fig. 7.05

The preceding code will replace {0} with the second argument, {1} with the third, and so on, up to {4} (the fifth string-replace argument). This does **not** work with `gs.logMessage()` or `gs.logError()`.

Did you remove your test logs before production?

Personally, I recommend using `gs.debug()` as opposed to `gs.log()` for *most* of your test-logging during development. There are a few reasons for this, but one of them is that if you forget to remove a log from your code, it won't clutter up the logs in production unless you've enabled debugging (as opposed to `gs.log()`, which *will* clutter the production logs). However, even with `gs.debug()`, you should remove any **unnecessary** log statements from your code **prior** to closing your update set and promoting your code to higher environments. Using `gs.debug()` can be a great way to include lots of log data in your scripts (as long as it's useful data) but which you only want to be logged if you're debugging.

CODE DOCUMENTATION

*Not just **what**, but **how***

Ink is better than the best memory.
—Chinese proverb

I have no idea what's going on here.
—Developers everywhere

Documenting your code is arguably one of the most important things that you can do—Period. Even if your code doesn't work, well-documented code will allow another developer to at least understand what you were going for.

Nearly every time you write code, you should be **documenting** that code. This takes the form of leaving actual comments in and around your code, as well as being sure to write "self-documenting" code (more on that in the following sub-sections). It is important to do both!

"Code documentation" refers to explanatory text within your code. This generally takes three main forms, which we'll learn about in this chapter:

1. Your variable names, structure, and syntax
2. Comments within your code
3. Specialized comments called **JSDoc**

SELF-DOCUMENTING CODE

Self-documenting code is, at its core, a best-practice way of naming things so that it's clear what they contain and what they're going to be used for. This is the bare minimum that you should be doing in order to make your code clear, readable, and extensible.

Writing self-documenting code *doesn't* mean that you don't have to write any actual comments in your code! In fact, **most** code you write should have something explaining what it is and how it works, even if it's highly obvious, just so the next person to read it doesn't go down a rabbit hole, seeking non-existent complexity. Code comments and self-documenting code are two methods of documentation that work **together** to make your code easily readable and updatable.

Self-documenting code can be broken down into three main components:

- Structure
- Naming
- Syntax

STRUCTURE

Self-documenting code begins with a clear structural outline that makes sense and flows **logically**. This means breaking out major stand-alone and often-utilized functionality into **functions** that can be called using intelligently-chosen, clear, concise names. This applies especially for functionality which, when simply written out, isn't very clear. Take the following line of code for example:

```
var w = m/60/24/7*0.001;
```

Fig. 8.01

At a glance, it's not totally clear what's going on here. To make it clearer, we could re-write it like this:

```
var milSeconds = 3200000;
var weeks = getWeeksFromMS(milSeconds);
function getWeeksFromMS(milSeconds) {
```

```
var seconds = milSeconds * 0.001;
var minutes = seconds / 60;
var hours = minutes / 60;
var days = hours / 24;
var weeks = days / 7;
return weeks;
}
```

Fig. 8.02

This is a *much* more unambiguous, if not the most efficient, way of writing this function (at least in terms of keystrokes). As an alternative, let's add some code comments to the original code, to make things clearer without needing to perform so many separate operations, and initialize so many variables:

```
var milSeconds = 3200000; //3.2 million milliseconds
var weeks = getWeeksFromMS(milSeconds);

function getWeeksFromMS(milSeconds) {
    /*Multiply by 0.001 to get seconds, divide by 60 to
    get minutes, 60 again to get hours, then by 24 to
    get days, and by 7 to get weeks, which we return.*/
    return milSeconds * 0.001 / 60 / 60 / 24 / 7;
}
```

Fig. 8.03

In the above code, we use multiple code documentation methods to make our code both clear, and succinct. Not only have we added actual **comments** to our code to explain what it's doing, but we've broken out the functionality of converting milliseconds into weeks, into a separate **function** with a **name** that makes it clear what it does. This way, unless it isn't working, we can look at just the first **two lines** of our code and have a good idea of what's going on here.

We've seen how, by making our code more **functional** (moving functionality into intelligently named functions), we can make our code clearer. But there is another opportunity for *functionalizing* and clarifying our code, which involves functionalizing certain **conditional expressions**. Consider the following code for an example of how we might improve:

```
if (!g_form.getValue('needs_repair') &&
!g_form.getValue('needs_replacement')) {
    g_form.showFieldMsg(
        'additional_info',
        'Please clarify what action is required',
        'info',
        false
    );
}
```

Fig. 8.04

In the code above, the condition in the `if` block is not too terribly complex, but its use of the `&&` operator along with the `!` negator may be confusing. Instead, it might be clearer if we wrote it like so:[28]

```
if (!needsRepairOrReplacement()) {
    g_form.showFieldMsg(
        'additional_info',
        'Please clarify what action is required',
        'info',
        False
    );
}

function needsRepairOrReplacement() {
    return (
        g_form.getValue('needs_repair') !== '' ||
        g_form.getValue('needs_replacement') !== ''
    );
}
```

Fig. 8.05

Even though it's technically more lines of code, it's much clearer what's going on. We've **abstracted** the bother of checking each field individually into a function, so as long as that function acts as expected, we can treat it like a black box that always returns what we're looking for. Of course, you can't always communicate everything about how your function works just by the naming convention; and that's where JSDoc comes in (see the section on JSDoc a little later in this chapter).

In this case though, we can make things even more simplistic by replacing the function itself, with a **variable**, like so:

[28] *Making complicated, multi-argument function calls easier to read by breaking them down into multiple lines, is called "chopping down". It can often make your code easier to read, and allows you to document each arg independently more easily. It's the difference between this:*
```
someFunction(someArg, someVal, 3, false);
```
and this:
```
someFunction(
    someArg,  //explanation
    someVal,  //details
    3,        //what is this
    false     //why
);
```

```
var needsRepairOrReplacement =
(g_form.getValue('needs_repair') !== '' ||
g_form.getValue('needs_replacement') !== '');

if (!needsRepairOrReplacement) {
    g_form.showFieldMsg('additional_info', 'Please clarify
what action is required', 'info', false);
}
```

Fig. 8.06

One last piece of advice when it comes to self-documenting code structure, is to **group** your statements logically. One example of that, which you may be familiar with, is initialization of variables. In JavaScript, the **interpreter** always groups variable initialization at the top of the scope, so if we want our code to be written in a way that matches the way it'll execute, we group initialization at the beginning like so:

```
function howAreYa(myName) {
    var response;
    var greeting = 'Hello, ' + myName;
    var question = 'How are ya?';

    console.log(greeting);
    response = prompt(question);
    console.log('You said: ' + response);
}
```

Fig. 8.07

That extra line-break in the middle visually separates the variable initialization and declaration block from the actual functionality of alerting and prompting the user. That makes it much easier to read, update, and troubleshoot! It also more closely reflects how the code will *actually execute* in the user's browser and it's helpful to prevent initialization of variables inside loops and attempting to use uninitialized variables that would only have been initialized inside conditional blocks.

NAMING

In addition to what we discussed in the **Naming Conventions** section of this compendium, the way you name primitive variables, functions, and other objects can also contribute to how "self-documenting" your code is. Avoid using vague terms like "handle" or "manage". For example, handleGlideRecords() is a lot less obvious than `convertGlideRecordToObject()` (for which, by the way, there is an OOB API for in the `GlideRecordUtil` Class: `.toHashMap()`).

For your functions, make sure they do one specific thing, and name them using active verbs like `sendFile()` or `convertXML()`. Make sure to contain **just** that functionality inside that function. If you need to add more functionality, that's fine, but you should accomplish that by returning something from the first function, and then potentially passing that something into the next step function. There are exceptions to this rule (as with all rules), but it'll help you out a lot to be mindful of this standard.

An example of what to try to **avoid** would be something like this:

```
validateRecord(record);

function validateRecord(record) {
    var recordIsValid = record.isValid() && record.active;
    if (recordIsValid) {
        updateRecord(record);
    }
}
function updateRecord(record) {
    if (record.update('something')) {
        return true;
    }
}
```

Fig. 8.08

Pro-tip. *In JavaScript, as long as there's only one line that executes following a conditional statement (`if()`), you technically don't have to include the curly braces. However, we **strongly recommend** that you do anyway; first, because it's **much** easier to read this way, and second because it's much easier and less confusing to update the functionality by adding additional statements in the conditional code block when the curly braces already exist.*

In this example, our executing code calls a function: `validateRecord()`. This function then calls another function to **update** the record: `updateRecord()`; but in our main top-level code, we haven't called the `updateRecord()` function, so a developer would have to **search through this code** to find out when and how the record is being updated, if they noticed it at all! This code's behavior doesn't make sense at first glance because the `validateRecord()` function is not only validating the record, but updating it too – which is contraindicated by its name.

Instead, we should do something closer to this:

```
if (validateRecord(record)) {
    updateRecord(record);
```

```
}

function validateRecord(record) {
    return record.isValid() && record.getValue('active')
=== 'true';
}

function updateRecord(record) {
    if (record.update('reason for update')) {
        return true;
    }
    return false;
}
```

Fig. 8.09

As you can see, it's much easier to understand what's going on here without having to investigate each function individually for additional **undocumented** (or at least, not self-documenting) functionality. Imagine if you look into function **a**, and learn that it uses function **b**, and function **b** uses function **c**, and so on. Tracing down the source of a bug in code like that would be a **nightmare**!

Note: *In the above code, as with most code samples in this document, we're not including **JSDoc** documentation, and may not be following one or two other best-practices. That's because I want to keep my sample code **succinct**, easy to read quickly, and to highlight the specific point that the sample is meant to demonstrate. Please do not model your code precisely off any one snippet of sample code here. Instead, focus on the specific lesson it's trying to demonstrate.*

Another good practice when it comes to naming variables, is to indicate the units of the variable. For example, instead of time, consider using timeInSeconds, or widthPx instead of width.

SYNTAX

When it comes to syntax, different coding languages have different syntactical tricks you can use. A few of these are mostly common knowledge and can make your code clearer. For example, **ternary** statements can be very useful if used only in the correct circumstances (and not chained, which can make them quite confusing). Ternary statements use ternary operators (? and :) to perform the same function as a simple conditional block, like so:

```
isValidRecord ? updateRecord() : logWarning('Record
invalid');
```

Fig. 8.10

The above code essentially says "If `isValidRecord` is true, then call `updateRecord()`. Otherwise, call `logWarning()`".

By the same token though, some syntactical tricks are more **arcane**, less well-known, and less supported. It's a good idea to avoid tricks like this. For example:

```
isValidRecord && updateRecord();
```

Instead, it's **usually** best to stick with the more clear, compatible, and common syntax (even if it's a bit more verbose). The following code does exactly the same thing as the preceding line does:

```
if (isValidRecord) {
    updateRecord();
}
```
Fig. 8.11

CODE COMMENTS

In addition to writing self-documenting code, it is important to leave **comments** in your code, indicating what's going on; especially when it otherwise might not be totally clear. Most scripts you write should contain **some** comments.

If you leave a code comment that is long enough to wrap to the next line, consider placing it in a "block-comment" above the code to which it applies, and using a manual line-break to wrap it, as in the following:

```
/*
This is a block comment about what the below
function does, and what it returns into the
hasThingBeenDone variable.
*/
var hasThingBeenDone = doAThing();
```
Fig. 8.12

You might also do a manual line-break before the line of code auto-wraps, and putting the next line in a separate comment using `//`. This is usually more readable, which is what code comments are all about!

Consider ways to make effective use of comments (and **well-named** variables) to make your code clearer. Consider the following line of code:

```
gr.addEncodedQuery('active=true^assignment_group=fe7204496
fd15e00b7e659212e3ee4e1^additional_assignee_listLIKE536968
cd6f9b21008ca61e250d3ee4d1');
```

Fig. 8.13

This doesn't make it very clear what we're doing, because as a developer looking at this code in 2 years, I'm not going to know what the sys_id values correspond to; but what if we wrote it out like this instead:

```
//Group: ServiceNow Dev Team
var assignmentGroup = 'fe7204496fd15e00b7e659212e3ee4e1';
//Assignee: John D Smith
var assignee = '536968cd6f9b21008ca61e250d3ee4d1';
var incidentQuery = 'active=true^assignment_group=' +
assignmentGroup + '^additional_assignee_listLIKE' +
assignee;

gr.addEncodedQuery(incidentQuery);
```

Fig. 8.14

This way is more verbose, but much more clear, and it gives us an opportunity to document what each sys_id corresponds to.

Note: Hard-coding Sys IDs is often not a good idea. Sometimes it's unavoidable, but if you can extrapolate or programmatically determine the record you want the sys_id for, this is usually better. Consider having an **assignee**'s Sys ID hard-coded in scripts throughout a workflow, and then the person to whom that Sys ID corresponds, leaves the company! Something like a **System Property** would usually be a better choice in cases like this, so you can modify it in just one place!

JSDOC

JSDoc is a **standards-based markup language** used to annotate JavaScript source code. Using comments containing JSDoc, you can add documentation describing the interface(s) of the code you're creating. This can then be processed by various tools, to produce documentation in accessible formats like HTML and Rich Text Format.

While ServiceNow does not currently support *Intellisense* or auto-completion based on JSDoc comments, many developers build their code in a more advanced external linter/IDE such as Jetbrains' Webstorm. JSDoc is supported in most such IDEs. Even when you're just building it in the default ServiceNow IDE though, JSDoc comments can be extremely helpful for "future-you", and for other developers, to understand how to interface with your code at a glance. I strongly recommend it for **Script Includes** which may be called from within various different types of scripts.

It certainly isn't required to JSDoc-ument *every* function or object in your code, but it is very strongly recommended for complex functions, especially ones in Script Includes.

Here is an example of **JSDoc** usage:

```
var TimeZoneUtils = Class.create();
TimeZoneUtils.prototype = {

    /**
    * Upon initialization, you can pass in a
GlideDateTime object you've already created and set to a
specific time.
    * The reference to this object will be used, and your
GDT will be modified in-place. Alternatively, you may
choose
    * not to specify a parameter upon initialization, and
a new GlideDateTime object will be created, used, and
returned
    * with the current time in the specified time-zone.
    *
    * @param {GlideDateTime} [gdt] - A reference to the
(optional) GlideDateTime object to be modified IN-PLACE.
    * If not specified, a new one will be generated, and
a reference returned.
    */
    initialize: function(gdt) {
        if (gdt) {
            this.gdt = gdt;
        } else {
            this.gdt = new GlideDateTime();
        }
    },

    /**
    * Get the GlideDateTime object (as a reference).
    * This will return a *reference* to the GlideDateTime
object. Note that because of JavaScript's
    * pass-by-reference jive, you should expect that if
you set a variable using this method, then
    * call another method which modifies the GDT object
referenced in this class, you will be modifying
    * the object to which your variable is a reference!
In other words, your variable will be modified *in-place*.
    * @returns {*|GlideDateTime}
    */
    getGDT: function() {
        return this.gdt;
    },
```

```
    /* OTHER STUFF HERE - THIS IS JUST AN EXAMPLE */

    type: 'TimeZoneUtils'
};
```

Fig. 8.15

You   can   find   more   info   on   JSDoc,   at   www.usejsdoc.org.

PERFORMANCE

Taking it to eleven

*Time dilation occurs at relativistic speeds as well as
in the presence of intense gravitational fields, and
while waiting for a webpage to load.*
—*This chapter quote*

I'm So Meta, Even This Acronym
—*I.S.M.E.T.A. (XKCD 917)*

PERFORMANCE IS IMPORTANT. Whether it comes in the form of query efficiency, database table configuration, or default layouts, building something that people are going to enjoy using, means building something that's fast.

It's tempting to include all the features and fields and really fancy logic and queries to add a bit of chrome to your application or solution, but every business knows that the **value** of everything should be considered in the context of its **cost**. Every person-hour spent waiting for a page to load or for a query to complete has a financial cost, as well as a cost that can be most effectively measured in Average-Rage-Per-Human, or ARPH. You want to keep your ARPH low, and your efficiency high.

QUERY EFFICIENCY

It's important to be **efficient** when querying the database (which includes GlideRecord queries). To that end, this section contains some basic guidelines for making sure your queries are efficient.

Inefficient database operations can be the source of a multitude of performance woes, including client-side issues like fields taking a long time to update, or the browser locking up when you perform certain sections – and server-side issues, such as lists, forms, and dashboards simply taking a long time to load. Most commonly, the culprit is one (or many) inefficient or non-optimized queries.

We've already gone over how to improve client-side performance by using asynchronous queries or other database, server, and API calls. In this section, we're going to learn how to write **queries** in such a way that there is an "as-minimal-as-possible" performance hit.

QUERY SPECIFICITY

You should generally try to make your queries as **specific** as possible. For example, if you only do something with the records returned from your query *in the event* that a specific condition is true, then that condition should be **part of the query**!

Consider the following code:

```
var grIncident = new GlideRecord('incident');
grIncident.addActiveQuery();
grIncident.query();
while (grIncident.next()) {
    if (grIncident.getValue('state') === '3') {
        gs.print('Incident ' +
grIncident.getValue('number') + ' is in state: 3.');
    }
}
```

Fig. 9.01

In this example, our database query would be monumentally more efficient if we were to add the condition currently in the `if` block, to the query itself, like so:

```
var grIncident = new GlideRecord('incident');
grIncident.addActiveQuery();
grIncident.addQuery('state', '3');
grIncident.query();
```

```
while (grIncident.next()) {
    gs.print('Incident ' + grIncident.getValue('number') +
' is in state 3.');
}
```

Fig. 9.02

There; that's **much** better!

SINGLE-RECORD QUERIES

Any time you use an `if` block rather than a loop (such as **if** `(gr.next())` `{}` rather than **while** `(gr.next())` `{}`), that means you're only looking for **one** record. The most efficient way to do this is to use the GlideRecord `.get()` API, and pass in a single argument: a **sys_id** or an **encoded query**. If it is not possible to specify a sys_id, there is a server-side version of the `.get()` API which can accept a query instead of a sys_id. However, due to the difference in client and server-side APIs, and for readability, it might be best to use `.setLimit()` instead, whenever you can't specify a sys_id. Also, when a sys_id is *not* specified to the `.get()` API, it may return multiple records – which can be confusing if you expect only one record, and also has a deleterious impact on performance, since the query continues after finding one record, to see if it can find more. For these reasons, it's often a good idea to just stick with using `.setLimit(1)`.

You can use `gr.setLimit(1)` to tell the database to stop searching after the first record is found. Otherwise, this would be like continuing to search for your keys, after you've found them. By the same token, if you are only expecting (or if you only *want*) a certain maximum number of records to be found, be sure to use `.setLimit()` to make the query easier on the database, and improve performance. Failing to set a limit on your query (or use the `.get()` API) will cause the database to continue searching the **entire table** that you've specified, even after it's found what it was looking for.

NESTED QUERIES

It's a good idea to avoid using **nested queries** if at all possible. This is because nested queries usually require a separate "inner" query for every single loop of the "outer" query, and can almost always be written more efficiently.

Nested queries are often incorrectly used when one needs to perform one query based on the records found based on another query.

Consider the following code:

```
var grUser;
var grIncident = new GlideRecord('incident');
grIncident.addEncodedQuery('some_query'); //include a
query param for 'assigned_to not blank'
grIncident.query();
while (grIncident.next()) {
    grUser = new GlideRecord('sys_user');
    if (grUser.get(grIncident.getValue('assigned_to'))) {
      //do something with the user
    }
}
```

Fig. 9.03

As you can see in the preceding code block, this would result in a **separate query** for each record returned from the "outer" query on the Incident table. If you get 10,000 Incidents from the outer query, that'll result in **10,000 separate queries** on the *sys_user* table (10,001 total, including the Incident query)!

As you might imagine, 10,001 separate queries could take quite some time. Instead, it would be dramatically more efficient if we were to use the first query to build a list of *sys_user* records we want to get from the database, then do a single query to get all of them. Rather than **10,001** queries, we're just doing two! Even though we're getting just as many records as the previous queries, we're doing so in one fell swoop, rather than going back-and-forth to the database to get each record.

Consider the following code as an example of dramatically improved efficiency:

```
var grUser, assignIDs = [];
var grInc = new GlideRecord('incident');
grInc.addEncodedQuery('some_query^asigned_to!=NULL');
grInc.query();
while (grInc.next()) {
    //This condition keeps the array values unique
    if (assignIDs.indexOf(grInc.getValue('assigned_to') <
0)) {
        assignIDs.push(grInc.getValue('assigned_to'));
    }
}

grUser = new GlideRecord('sys_user');
grUser.addQuery('sys_id', 'IN', assignIDs);
/*Include any other query params here, such as if you
only want to return active users.
Note that it is more efficient to add those query
params here, rather than via dot-walking on the
Incident table query, because dot-walking inside
of one query effectively results in a separate
query on the dot-walked table (which we're doing
```

```
here, anyway!)*/
grUser.query();
while (grUser.next()) {
    //NOW do something with the assignee records
}
```
Fig. 9.04

Note: *Although I didn't want to break the flow of the example code, it would actually be far more efficient to use* GlideAggregate *and the* .groupBy() *API for the first query in the preceding example, because we only need the unique* assigned_to *values!*

There is one down-side to the preceding example: When you do the second query, you lose the "context" of the Incident to which the user was assigned, because we didn't put that data into our array. This can make things difficult, if the action we want to take on the user record is *dependent* on some data in the Incident. Not to worry though, you can easily remedy this by storing this data in an **object** rather than an **array**!

In the example code below, we'll construct an object from each Incident returned from the first query, and use the data in that object to do the work in our second query:

```
var inc, incAssignedToUser, grUser, assignID, incID;
var assignData = {};
var grIncident = new GlideRecord('incident');
grIncident.addEncodedQuery('some_query^assigned_to!=NULL')
;
grIncident.query();
while (grIncident.next()) {
    incID = grIncident.getValue('sys_id');
    assignID = grIncident.getValue('assigned_to');
    /*If the assignee has not been added to the
    assignData object, create it.*/
    if (!assignData[assignID]) {
        assignData[assignID] = {};
    }
    /*Create an object inside the assignee object in
    the assignData object, to hold the incident
    data (using the Incident() ES5 constructor)*/
    assignData[assignID][incID] = new
Incident(grIncident);
}

grUser = new GlideRecord('sys_user');
grUser.addQuery('sys_id', 'IN', Object.keys(assignData));
grUser.query();
while (grUser.next()) {
    for (inc in assignData[grUser.getValue('sys_id')]) {
```

```
    //Check if property is enumerable
        if (assignData.hasOwnProperty(inc)) {
            incAssignedToUser =
assignData[grUser.getValue('sys_id')][inc];
            //NOW do something with the user/incident pair
        }
    }
}

/**
 * @param grIncident {GlideRecord}
 * @constructor
 */
function Incident(grIncident) {
    this.sys_id = grIncident.getValue('sys_id');
    this.number = grIncident.getValue('number');
    //etc...
}
```

Fig. 9.05

This code uses a constructor function (`Incident()`) to generate a structured object from the `grIncident` GlideRecord object, to store all of the data about the Incident that we might need to use later. In this way, we're "building a to-do list" which we then leverage in our second query. In order to keep our second query efficient and limit it to just the records we know we'll need to interact with, we use `Object.keys(assignData)`, which returns an array of the keys in the `assignData` object (which you may have noticed, are the sys_ids of the assignees in question!)

Granted, the preceding code is... quite a lot longer than the first, or second examples. However, it is also a **lot** more efficient, and provides whatever additional context you need from the Incident records, when working with the user/assignee records.

Pro-tip. Should you need to, you can get an array of the sys_ids to which a specific user is assigned in the final `while` loop, using something like:

```
Object.keys(assignData[grUser.getValue('sys_id')])
```

QUERY ORDER

It's important to realize – especially when dealing with very large or poorly optimized tables – that the **order** of your queries matters. I'm not talking about the GlideRecord `.orderBy()` method; I'm talking about the order in which you add your query filters.

Note: *The instance **caches** the results of a query for extremely quick subsequent retrieval, and once cached, the order of query parameters is much less important. However, it's still important to write our queries for **maximum efficiency**!*

According to a community post by one of our contributors, JarodM, you can reduce your query time by up to or even over **90%** on the first query after instance cache is cleared by following a few simple steps to ensure your queries are ordered properly.

You can see the post we're referring to at http://performancepost.snc.guru/.

To understand why your query order matters, consider the following scenario:

Say you have 1,000 records in the Incident table: 900 **inactive** records, and 100 **active** records. Imagine you'd like to get all **active** Incidents where the **Short description** field contains the phrase "oh god, why is this happening".

The work of checking whether the **active** field is **true** is really quite easy, but the work of checking whether a string "**contains**" another string can be (comparatively speaking) much more costly. For that reason, in the above scenario, it would make sense to put the **active** query **first** and the **contains** query **second**. The reason that this is more performance-friendly, is that the first query – being **less computationally intensive** – filters out 90% of the records that you have to do the *more* computationally intensive **contains** query on.

Pro-tip: *There is a quick-and-easy* <u>server-side</u> *GlideRecord API for adding an active query. Rather than writing* `gr.addQuery('active', 'true')`, *you can use the simpler* `gr.addActiveQuery()`. *There does not appear to be any performance benefit to this, however.*

To simplify this into a general rule: Always try to put the **less computationally intensive** query filters **first**, so you have to do the more intensive operations on fewer records to filter your results.

MULTI-RECORD OPERATIONS

Imagine you need to write a scheduled script that'll **close** all Incidents which are in the **In Progress** state, if they haven't been updated within the last **30 days**. One way to do this would be to use a query to show only those records, and loop through every record we find, to make our changes. That code might look something like this:

```
var grStaleIncident = new GlideRecord('incident');
grStaleIncident.addEncodedQuery('active=true^state=2^sys_u
pdated_onRELATIVELE@dayofweek@ago@30');
grStaleIncident.query();
while (grStaleIncident.next()) {
  //state 7 is 'Closed'
    grStaleIncident.setValue('state', '7');
    grStaleIncident.update();
}
```

Fig. 9.06

The preceding code would work just fine, but let's think about the individual transactions that are occurring here.

1.   First, we query each record from the database to the server on which the script is running.
2.   Next, on the server, we iterate over each of the returned records, make a change to it, and send that record back to the database using the .update() API.
3.   Then we iterate into the next record, do the same change again, and send that one record back to the database server.

This repeats for every single record that's returned from our query.

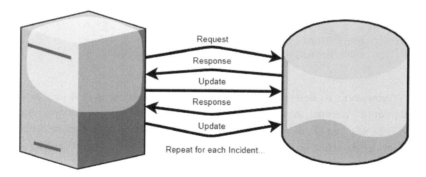

The vast majority of this "back-and-forth" can be avoided, using a **multi-record operation**. In the above case, we're updating the exact same fields with the exact same values, on every single record returned from our query. Instead, we could just send the database a query, and tell it: "everything that matches this query – set these fields to these values".

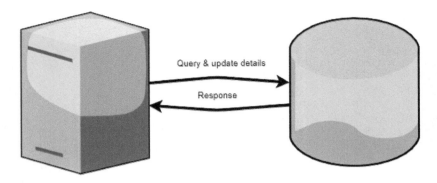

Query & update details

Response

This is much more efficient because it tells the database server all the work we want to do, and lets it get on with it, without having to return the result to the server our script is running on, and wait for the next update on the next record. Even though the scripting server and the database server have an exceptionally fast connection, these "back-and-forth" transactions do have a cost!

Back to our example in the preceding code snippet: here is how we could rewrite that code to use the multi-record API: .updateMultiple().

```
var grStaleIncident = new GlideRecord('incident');
grStaleIncident.addEncodedQuery('active=true^state=2^sys_u
pdated_onRELATIVELE@dayofweek@ago@30');
//state 7 is 'Closed'
grStaleIncident.setValue('state', '7');
grStaleIncident.updateMultiple();
```
Fig. 9.07

If you want to **delete** all records matching a specific query, just as before, you could iterate over each record in a while(){} loop, and call .deleteRecord() on each one. However, it would be much more efficient to just let the database do the work for you in a multi-record operation like so:

```
var gr = new GlideRecord('incident');
gr.addEncodedQuery(someQuery);
gr.deleteMultiple();
```
Fig. 9.08

There are a couple of **important notes** to be aware of when dealing with multi-record operations:
- You should already be doing this anyway, but **always** use .setValue(), rather than directly setting the field object like gr.short_description = 'some value';.

- o Failure to do this with a multi-record operation can result in it **ignoring your query/filter**, and performing the operation on all records in your table!
- Don't use multi-record operations on tables with **currency** type fields.
  - o I have no idea why this is, but ServiceNow's documentation warns against it. It seems to cause the whole thing to fail.

Don't use multi-record operations with the `.setLimit()`, or `.chooseWindow()` APIs. It will ignore them.

CREATING/INSERTING RECORDS

Along with deleting records, **inserting** new records is one of the more strenuous database operations you can perform. It is therefore important to make sure that you're **maximizing efficiency** wherever possible when it comes to inserting records. One common mistake that developers make when creating database records through code, is to treat the GlideRecord `.newRecord()` API method as interchangeable with `.insert()`.

The `.newRecord()` method is actually different from `.initialize()` in some significant ways. `.newRecord()` generates a new sys_id value, as well as values for any "default" or "auto-number" fields (such as the number field on the task table(s)). This means that each `.newRecord()` call requires a database transaction; unlike `.initialize()`.

```
//The slower way, but lines 4 and 5 work.
var grIncident = new GlideRecord('incident');
grIncident.newRecord(); //MUCH slower than .initialize()!
gs.info(grIncident.getValue('sys_id')); //(some sys_id)
gs.info(grIncident.getValue('number')); //INC0010098
```

The `.initialize()` API method is MUCH faster due to not requiring any back-and-forth with the database to perform its function. The only potential down-side is that your "initialized" GlideRecord object will not contain any of the values that would be determined or calculated on the server, such as sys_id, auto-number fields, or fields with default values.

```
//Much faster, but lines 4 and 5 won't work.
var grIncident = new GlideRecord('incident');
grIncident.initialize(); //Much faster, but breaks the
below two lines.
```

```
gs.info(grIncident.getValue('sys_id')); //null
gs.info(grIncident.getValue('number')); //null
```

It's worth pointing out though, that these missing auto-generated and default values will **still be generated once the record is inserted** (assuming you haven't set the fields with default values in your code). They simply won't be available to you in your code unless you use `.newRecord()`. It's quite rare that you should need to access these sorts of values in your code, though; therefore, the `.initialize()` method is highly preferable the vast majority of the time.

TABLES & LISTS

In another chapter of this compendium, we learned about the negative impact of adding unnecessarily large fields to a database table (especially a base table like **Task** [*task*]). But consider that it's also costly in terms of performance, to add such long fields to a form or list view. Even if these fields are **hidden** on the form, their contents **must still be retrieved** from the server and sent to the client. For especially long fields, this can have a noticeable impact on the form's load-time. For this reason, it's a good idea to avoid putting fields on the form if they don't need to be there; and the same goes for lists.

Another thing to consider, is how your lists are **ordered**. Ordering a large list by a field that isn't **indexed** can have significant performance impacts. This performance cost is even greater for fields that have a higher computational cost to order, such as a non-indexed **date/time** field.

*Pro-tip. Many users complain about how slow ServiceNow is when they first log in, but you'll often notice that these long transactions are caused by them loading their **homepage**. A homepage can consist of widget-after-widget containing large, poorly-optimized lists with poorly optimized queries, data visualizations, and so on. It might be a good idea to enable a default **blank** homepage user preference in the **sys_user_preference** table.*

LARGE DATABASE OPERATIONS

There will be plenty of perfectly valid situations in which you need to perform very large database operations. Most often, these operations are "one-offs", meaning that you only need to do them one time. For example, re-classifying a large number of CIs. This operation is pretty heavy on its own, but it can also trigger a large number of cascade operations (and it is typically not wise to use `.setWorkflow(false)` on such operations).

Unfortunately, these large operations can often take a *very* long time (days, even!) and can bump up against certain limitations – SQL database limits, transaction time limits, script execution time limits, etc. These limits can be extended to a point, but it's not a great idea to extend those limits to the extremes that would be required for such large operations. So, what's a developer to do? – Calm down, I was just about to tell you!

EVENT-DRIVEN RECURSION

Event-driven recursion operations (or EDR ops) are a way to approach solving the problem of having to perform a large number of heavy database operations using a single thread, without worrying about database or transaction limitations.

I go into some detail on this point in the Free Tools & Articles chapter of this book, so I won't repeat myself here (gotta keep the book DRY[29], right?); but I wanted to reference the solution, since it's also relevant in this chapter section.

EDR can even be combined with the next solution (multi-threading), as you'll see in the next section!

You can read up on this topic and see some example code in that chapter, or in my detailed article on the topic at https://edr.snc.guru.

MULTI-THREADING

Event-driven recursion is a pattern specifically designed to **avoid bogging down your instance**; even stepping aside between each iteration, to allow the event queue to clear out before moving on to the next iteration.

This is great for performance, but sometimes you just need to get the job done as quickly as possible!

Multi-threading[30] is the exact opposite; its purpose is to break down the work into a bunch of smaller chunks, and then throw them all (or some subset of them) at the database at once to get the job done as quickly as possible. This *usually* isn't quite as bad for performance as it may initially seem, so long as

---

[29] *Get it? -- GET IT?!*

[30] *Note that it's entirely possible to **combine** multi-threading with event-driven recursion, since EDR will only execute one thread per sub-batch.*

you're not doing this during business hours or while the database is already taxed. The ServiceNow database is quite a lot faster than the application server node. Therefore, you can send off several jobs to the database from the app server in separate threads and get around the application server node bottleneck.

The way to trigger multiple threads is simple; just create multiple **Scheduled Jobs**, each set to execute **on demand**, and then click **Execute now** on the ones you want to run. The hard part will be effectively breaking up the job into batches that have **zero overlap**.

Avoiding overlap between your threads is very important, because of a concept in computer science called "thread collision". This happens when multiple threads – multiple simultaneously executing bits of code – are attempting to access the same "resource" (in this case, the resources are specific records). If your threads (that is, your **scheduled jobs**) don't have separate queries which uniquely identify records that are theirs, and only theirs, to work with, multiple threads may simultaneously attempt to update a single record at the same time (or even one after another). This is usually a bad thing.

One way to avoid having overlap in your threads, is to write your query using the sys_created_on field and give each thread (scheduled job) a block of time[31]; for example, in increments of something like 3, 6, or 12 months.

You may also consider using the sys_id field, break your query down into 2, 4, 8, or 16 chunks. Since sys_ids are **hexadecimal** values, they use the decimal digits 0-9, as well as the alpha characters a-f. Since that's 16 total possible characters, you can split your query into two batches where the first query gets all records where the sys_id begins with the numbers 0-7, and the second query gets all records with a sys_id beginning with the number 8, 9, *or* the letters a-f. To split it into four batches/threads, you'd have each thread handle sys_ids beginning with one of the following sets: (*0-3*), (*4-7*), (*8, 9, a, or b*), and (*c-f*). Hopefully you can see how to divide the sets further; even into more than 16 batches, if you use a "starts with" query and the first *two* characters of the sys_id rather than just the first one.

UNNECESSARY LOG STATEMENTS

---

[31] *If you use this method, make sure to hard-code the date/times you're using without any overlap. Using something like* javascript:gs.daysAgo(7) *in your query may result in overlap, since you won't be able to execute all of the scheduled jobs simultaneously down to the second.*

One last note on performance. Logging doesn't just happen in code. Every single log statement results in a database INSERT transaction, into a very heavily taxed and utilized table. In addition to cluttering up your logs, making it more difficult to identify meaningful logs when you actually need to troubleshoot something.

If you're logging from your code, and you don't actually *need* the logs to show up, consider switching to a `gs.debug()` statement, which only fires if debug logging is enabled in your instance/application.[32] Better yet, use the debugger instead![33] Leaving `gs.log()` statements in the final code that you promote to production, should be an *extremely rare thing*, and should only be done when *necessary*.

CONFIGURABILITY

Let them decide how your code

works

gs.getProperty('chapter_quote', '');
—Chuck Norris

THE SERVICENOW PLATFORM is highly configurable. You might even say that that's one of, if not *the*, biggest draw of the platform: the ability to customize and configure it to do nearly anything you can imagine. As much as many organizations advocate for "low-code" or "no-code" solutions (and as much as ServiceNow has done to make these sorts of customizations possible), most advanced customizations to the platform (custom apps, integrations, alterations to existing functionality, etc.) still require *actual development*.

There is *nothing wrong with actual development*! The ability to sling some code and make the system do exactly what you want it to do, is arguably the primary reason that ServiceNow has become the ubiquitous "everything platform" used by 75% of Fortune 500s! But with great power comes great responsibility; in this case, the responsibility to think carefully about the solutions you're building, before you ever put digital pen to metaphorical paper. This is one a critical role of the technical architect, but it's a concept that any senior-level developer should be familiar with.

In this chapter, we're going to talk about an aspect of technical architecture that's important for both technical architects *and* developers to understand: architecting and building your applications with configurability in mind. We're going to learn about:

- How to think about configurability in the context of ServiceNow

- How to determine what functionality it makes sense to make configurable
- Getting the business to identify areas that they may want to change – "levers" they may want to pull, to alter the functionality of the tool – at the architecture phase.
- How to actually build functionality with modularity in mind, using **system properties** and **user preferences**
- How to define "default" user preferences, and how to specify meaningful defaults for missing system properties.
- How to build useful and informative "settings" pages for your tools and functionality, to provide a positive user experience
- Controlling access to the settings for your functionality, to avoid unauthorized/accidental changes to the functionality.

PLANNING FOR CONFIGURABILITY

When thinking about how you're going to build out your solution, it's important to ask yourself (and maybe your stakeholders) several questions first:

1. Are there any pieces of this functionality that we *know* will need to change after we build this?
    a. This includes things like credentials, endpoints, API keys, and any tweaks which may need to be made to enable "test mode".
2. Is there any specific behavior of the application which you think your stakeholders might be likely to change their minds about, or want to configure/tweak over time?
    a. For example, imagine you're writing a UI action that should appear on all tables that meet some criteria (such as my "Include in Update Set" tool: http://include.snc.guru/). In that case, you may want to have a system property that contains exclusions. Even if you don't have any exclusions to begin with, it'll give you a way to add them!
3. Is there any situation where you might need to switch the functionality on or off?
    a. Also consider whether it's conceivable that your functionality could cause a problem that could only discovered in production. If so, it's extremely handy to have a "master on/off switch" that you can simply toggle off while you work up a patch!

In each case, when deciding whether to make a "setting" for your app, it's important to think carefully about whether this should be a user-configurable setting (set on a user-by-user basis, using "user preferences"), or whether it should be a system-wide setting (using "system properties").

By planning out your functionality with configurability in-mind, you'll save yourself a lot of time and hassle down the line. What's more, you'll look like an *absolute boss* when someone says "hey, is there anyway we could make this tool do [something] instead of how it currently works?" and you can immediately reply "Sure, I built it that way because I'm a freakin' mind-reader. It'd take me 10 seconds to make it do that."

SYSTEM PROPERTIES

The most common and approachable way to make your tool or functionality configurable, is using **system properties**. System properties are just records in the *sys_properties* table. Instead of doing a GlideRecord query though, you'll use `gs.getProperty()`[34] to get a system property's value, or `gs.setProperty()`[35] to set its value.

System properties are a great way to control system-wide behaviors, but they should not be used to control user-specific behaviors. For that, we have user preferences (discussed later in this chapter).

All of that said, be aware that while you can retrieve system property values willy-nilly with near-zero performance impact, **setting** system property values can result in some performance issues in your instance! Unless the property record corresponding to the setting (in the *sys_properties* table) has the **Ignore cache** field set to true, any time you set or update the value of a system property, it triggers a system cache flush! For this reason, it's important to try not to use system properties for any settings which may need to be updated frequently. If the setting might need to be updated *somewhat frequently*, then be sure to at least set the **Ignore cache** checkbox field to true (keeping in mind that this may cause issues – you wouldn't want to do this, for example, on your master on/off switch property!)

When retrieving the value of a system property using `gs.getProperty()`, the first argument should be the property name, but there is an optional second parameter which, I would argue, you should *almost always use*! If you make a habit of using this second argument whenever you call `gs.getProperty()` and you're ever in a situation where the property has been marked as private and not deployed, has been deleted, or by whatever other mechanism might be inaccessible, you'll have a "default value" built-in whenever you call it, so your code won't abjectly break.

Another thing to keep in mind when retrieving a system property value with `gs.getProperty()`, is that it will **always return a string**. Consider the following:

```
var propIsTen = gs.getProperty('my_prop', 10) === 10;
```
Fig. 10.01

---

[34] `gs.getProperty()` *is a server-side method, and cannot be used from within client-side scripts. You can build a simple client-callable Script Include that would allow you to get a system property value by name, using GlideAjax. Better yet, whenever possible, use a "display" Business Rule to add the property value to the "scratchpad"* `(g_scratchpad)`

[35] *When using* `gs.setProperty()`, *if the property doesn't already exist, it'll create it. If you specify a second argument, the description of the property will be set to whatever you specify there!*

If your system property does indeed have a value of *10*, the above statement will **still return false**, because `gs.getProperty()` will return a string, but the above statement is strictly comparing the returned value with an integer (*10*). This is true even if the *"my_prop"* system property doesn't exist, and `gs.getProperty()` returns the "default" value that we specified in the second argument, which is an integer. It will **cast that integer to a string** before returning it! For this reason, I recommend **always specifying a string as the second argument** when calling `gs.getProperty()`. Otherwise, you risk unexpected behavior as a result of the type-coercion that happens before the default value is returned (as a string).

SYSTEM PROPERTY CATEGORIES

Once you've got some **system properties** created to control system-wide settings for your application, tool, or functionality, you'll want to display them in some sort of cohesive interface. This will provide a veritable "single pane of glass" for viewing and configuring the settings related to your functionality.

To group the settings related to a specific application or set of functionality, you'll want to add them to a **System Properties Category** [*sys_properties_category*]. The way to associate a system property to a system property category, is by adding a record to an intermediary many-to-many ("M2M") table, called **Category Properties** [*sys_properties_category_m2m*]. With that done, you *could* swing for the fences and build your own custom portal page to display a "settings" interface for all of your system properties, but the *easiest* (and most common) way to display your system properties is by using the *system_properties_ui.do* UI page. You can easily load a given system properties category in that UI page by navigating to the category, and clicking on the "**Try it**" UI Action.

Try It

Clicking on the "Try it" UI Action will take you to the *system_properties_ui.do* UI page, but you'll notice that the browser tab has no meaningful title, and the word "null" shows up in the header where you'd expect a title to be.

null   Save

To resolve this, copy the URL of the page that opened up when you clicked "Try it", and then let's add an additional URL parameter: *sysparm_title*. Let's say we want to add the title "Example Properties" to that settings page. To do that, just append *&sysparm_title=Example%20Properties*[36] to the end of the URL for the page that opened, and put that new URL in your browser's URL bar. Now, you'll notice that the title is shown in the browser tab, as well as in the page header!

Example Properties   Save

Now, you can simply create an **application navigator module** that points to that URL, to display the settings of your application! Even as you add new properties to that category, they will show up on that settings page automatically.

Finally, just like with system properties, keep in mind that the **Description** field of a system properties category accepts rich text/HTML, and will be rendered on the page when someone clicks your settings module!

Note: While system properties categories have a ***rich-text*** Description field, the Description field on the System Properties themselves is just a plain-text field. That said, you can still enter HTML, and it'll render just fine on the page!

USER PREFERENCES

System Properties are great for controlling system-wide settings such as an on/off switch, but sometimes you want to allow users to adjust settings that only affect themselves and their own experience. For that, we can use **user preferences**! User preferences live in the **User Preferences** [*sys_user_preference*] table, and have only four **Types**: Integer, Reference, String, and True/False.

Unfortunately, unlike system properties, **user preferences** don't have a handy-dandy interface UI page out of the box. Most user-selected preferences are updated implicitly by actions taken through the ServiceNow UI, such as by clicking on a column header on the list view of a table to change the way that table is sorted. You could use similar techniques so that most of your user preferences are set implicitly and retained, but I can imagine at least a few scenarios in which you'd want your users to be able to manually set their preferences through a UI similar to that which we have for system properties.

---

[36]*Certain characters aren't allowed in a URL. The space character is one of these characters. In order to represent them in a URL, they must be encoded by a percent sign followed by a two-character code. The URL-encoded version of a space, is "%20", which is why you see "%20" between the words "Example" and "Properties" in this URL.*

For that, you may want to put together a UI page, category table, and preference-to-category m2m relationship table, based on the system properties UI page which allows you to set up and display user preference categories for your app, and display them to users so they can configure their own preferences.

SETTING USER PREFERENCES

There are situations where you may want to alter a given user preference as the result of a script running. For example, the **Make this my current update set** UI Action on Update Set records changes the user preference relating to the user's currently selected update set to the sys_id of the currently opened update set record. Luckily, ServiceNow provides both a client-side, and a server-side API for performing this update. **Client-side**, the API is:

```
setPreference('preference_name', 'preferece_value')
```

Server-side, you would use:

```
gs.getUser().setPreference('pref_name', 'pref_value')
```

Finally, you can also set a user preference by **navigating to a specially crafted URL**[37]! You can link a user to literally any page, and simply append a URI parameter called `sysparm_userpref.<preference_name>`, and set it to the new value of the user preference. This can be an extremely useful tool for allowing users to click a link and update a user preference without scripting; and it isn't just for custom preferences! For example, imagine a user has complained that they can no longer see the **Work notes** field on the Incident form. You believe that this is because they've configured their form to hide certain fields, (which, on the default view, is controlled by the "*personalize_incident_default*" user preference). Rather than walking them through the steps to find the "**Personalize form**" button and make sure that all the boxes are ticked, you can simply send them to the following URL and ask them if they can see the **Work notes** field now:

---

[37] *This functionality can be risky, as users can be tricked into clicking a link that sets list limits to a single record, or changes their colors or time-zone or various other things about how they experience the ServiceNow platform. For this reason, it may be wise to be judicious and think carefully if it would be possible for something to break in a very damaging way, if your user were to click a maliciously crafted URL that sets any user preferences you've created. It's also wise to always practice **defensive programming**, and just assume that there's every chance that when retrieving the value of a preference, you may get a broken, malformed, blank, or otherwise invalid value!*

```
https://<your_instance>.service-
now.com/incident.do?sys_id=-
1&sysparm_userpref.personalize_incident_default=
```

By putting no value after the equals-sign in that URL, we're effectively setting the value of the *personalize_incident_default* to blank, which means that the default value will be used, just as if the user preference were not set at all.

*Note: When setting a user preference in this way, the preference record is updated on the server **before** the page is loaded; otherwise, this would require that the user click the link and then load the page again!*

RETRIEVING USER PREFERENCES

To **retrieve** the value of a user preference in a script, you can use the following APIs:

Client-side:[38]
```
getPreference('preference_name');
```
Server-side:
```
gs.getPreference('preference_name', 'default_value');
```

Note that, unlike the server-side `gs.getPreference()` method, the client-side `getPreference()` function does *not* accept a second "default value" argument. Remember to always aim to practice "defensive programming", and make sure your code can handle null, blank, undefined, invalid, and unexpected values being returned from user preferences!

DEFAULT (GLOBAL) USER PREFERENCES

When defining a new User Preference to control some functionality on a user-by-user basis, you'll want to make sure that you have a **default** value[39] for that preference, so that if a user hasn't manually updated their preference, any attempts to retrieve its value will return whatever you've set as the default.

To create a default user preference, navigate to the **User Preferences** [*sys_user_preference*] table, and create a new record. Set the **Name** field to the

---

[38] Note that the client-side getPreference() API uses a **synchronous** AJAX call to the server, so – as you can probably guess from the *Performance* chapter of this handbook - I highly recommend that you use it only very sparingly or, better yet, write your own **asynchronous** GlideAjax or Scripted REST API (SRAPI) method!

[39] Default user preferences are also commonly referred to as "global" or "system" user preferences. Whenever you hear "system user preference" or "global user preference", just think "default".

name of the user preference you're going to have your users set. Leave the **User** field blank and check the **System** checkbox.

Note: You should never have more than one default (global/system) user preference with the same name. Each user preference should have one, and only one, default value.

User preferences are not included in Update Sets by default, **except if you check the "System" checkbox.** If you *do* check that box, your user preference record *will* be included in your Update Set. If you'd like to include **non-default** system properties in your Update Set, you'll need to use something like the SN Guys' **Include in Update Sets** tool to force the user preference record(s) into your Update Set. You can download this tool for free from SN Pro Tips, at http://include.snc.guru/

When retrieving the value of a user preference, the **default** value will only be returned if the user has no user-specific preference of the same name. Here's an example of how that would work:

1. You create a default user preference record by leaving the **User** field blank, and checking the **System** checkbox. You name this user preference *companyname_portal.header.bgcolor*. You set the value of this default preference to the hex code for dark blue.
2. On your company's service portal, you code the header so that it determines its background color by calling the `gs.getPreference()` API. You also set up a little color-picker menu, where clicking on one of the color options appends `sysparm_userpref.companyname_portal.header.bgcolor=<new_color>` argument to the URL, with its value set to the hex value of the selected color.
3. A user, Bob Smith, logs in and navigates to the portal for the first time. Since bob has no user-specific *sys_preference* record for the header's background color, the **default** value (dark blue) is used.
4. Bob clicks on the color-picker and selects a new color: pink. This appends a URI parameter to the page's URL, with its value set to the hex code for pink. This updates the value of the user preference record on the server before reloading the page, so when it does load, the call to the `gs.getPreference()` API returns the new value: the hex code for pink; and Bob sees the pink portal header that he's expecting.

SESSION VARIABLES & CLIENT DATA

Session variables and **client data** in ServiceNow are closely linked, but are not the exact same thing. Both are user-specific - similar to **user preferences** - but are less persistent than user preferences.

Session variables are (as the name implies) unique to a specific **user login session**[40]. This means that they're more *ephemeral* than **user preferences**, which persist between sessions after the user logs off and on again later (even from another location). **Client data**, meanwhile, is even less persistent. Client data only persists until you save a record or reload a page. In other words, session variables are linked with your session, on the server. Client data is linked with a specific instance of a page in the client (your web browser).

This non-persistence can be a good thing! You may for example, want the user to be able to alter something about their experience, but not have that change persist each time they log in. For example, perhaps you want to have the user select something on one page in your Service Portal which determines the behavior or contents of the next page. For this, you hypothetically *could* use a "user preference", but to do so would be overkill. It may even be *undesirable* to have that selection persist through multiple sessions.

I mentioned above that session variables and client data are closely linked. That's because every time you load a page or form, ServiceNow gets all of your server-side **session variables**, and sets a **client data element** from it. In other words, if you have a **session variable** called `last_selection` set to the value `12`, when you load a ServiceNow form, you can access that session variable as a **client data** element, just as you would any other.

There is one caveat, though: **it doesn't go both ways**. Setting a session variable on the server will make that variable (and its value) available on all future page loads[41] as client data, but setting a client data element will not cause that value to persist as a session variable on the server; even if the client data element you set, was originally derived from a server-side session variable. For example, if you were to set that `last_selection` session variable mentioned above and load a new page, you'd have a client data element with that same name and value. However, if you were to – in a **Client Script** – change the value of that client data from `12` to `7`, that change would persist *only until you reloaded the page*, at which point you would find that the value of that client data element reverted to the value of its corresponding session variable on the server (`12`).

Let's have a look at a real-world example of using session variables and client data. This example will be a little *contrived*, but just go with it.

---

[40] A "session" is essentially a specific instance of a user logging in. If you log in to your ServiceNow instance, that's one session. If you open a second tab, that second tab is still going to be logged into your first session. If, however, you load your instance in a new "incognito" window or in a separate browser, you will need to log in again. This constitutes a **new session**, which will have its own session ID. In this way, a single user can have multiple sessions, but no two users can share the same login session.

[41] Note that I said it'd be available on all **future** page loads. Setting a session variable on the server does not automatically update client data for any pages which were already loaded. That data only shows up on future page loads.

Let's say you've been tasked with the following requirement:

1. When a user **saves an Incident** to the database, if the **Category** field changes, get the **category** of that Incident, and save it to a **session variable**.
2. The next time a user loads the Incident "new record" form, the **Category** field should be set to the last category they saved an Incident with.

You might start by creating a Business Rule that runs on **Insert** or **Update**, whenever the **Category** field **Changes**. Since this BR doesn't need to modify anything about the record that triggers it, we'll make it an **After** Business Rule. Since we're going to need to write some code to set the session variable, we'll check the **Advanced** checkbox.

The initial configuration of our Business Rule might look something like this:

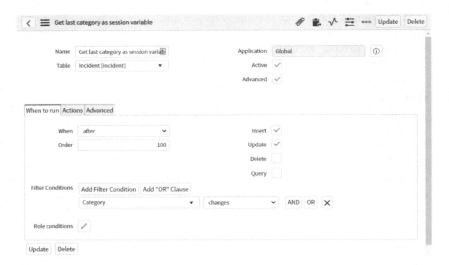

Next, we need to write the script to set the session variable on the server in that BR, so we'll switch over to the **Advanced** tab and write a script that looks something like this:

```
(function executeRule(current, previous /*null when
async*/) {
```

```
    var lastSelectedCategory =
current.getValue('category');
    gs.getSession().putClientData(
        'last_selected_category',
        lastSelectedCategory
    );

})(current, previous);
```

Fig. 10.02

The next step is to write a **Client Script** to access the client data element whenever the Incident "new record" form is loaded, and use it to set the value of the **Category** field. You may notice in the above script that if the category field is blank, then the last_selected_category session variable will also be blank. Because of this, our Client Script will also have to check whether that variable is set to a *truthy* value (like a non-blank string), before updating the Category field on the form.

We'll create an **onLoad** Client Script on the Incident table, set the **Type** to **All** so it'll run on portal and workspace pages as well, and use something like the following code:

```
function onLoad() {
    //Hoist variable declarations
    var isvalidCategory, lastSelectedCategory;
    //Prevent script from running unless we're on the "new
record" form.
    if (!g_form.isNewRecord()) {
        return;
    }
    lastSelectedCategory = g_user.getClientData(
        'last_selected_category'
    );
    //Halt if last selected category not set.
    if (!lastSelectedCategory) {
        return;
    }
    //Determine if last selected category is a valid.
    //Cast to boolean with !!.
    isvalidCategory = !!g_form.getOption(
        'category',
        lastSelectedCategory
    );
    if (isvalidCategory) {
        g_form.setValue('category', lastSelectedCategory);
    }
}
```

Fig. 10.03

In the above code, we're checking that we're on the new record form (line 5-7), getting the last selected category (ln 8-10), checking that `lastSelectedCategory` is set to a non-empty value (ln 12-14), checking that the value in `lastSelectedCategory` is a *valid choice* for the Category field (ln 17-20), and – if it is – setting the Category field value (ln 21-23). And that's all there is to it!

MODULARITY

Modularity, in the context of software, means breaking down a program or some functionality into smaller pieces with standardized interfaces; but writing modular code can mean more than just breaking it into pieces; it can mean making each individual piece modular, as well! In this section, we'll see how to write modular code with "smarter" interfaces using default parameters. We'll also learn how to create configuration records that allow you (or other application admins!) to control some limited aspects of your functionality, such as by transforming data on-the-fly, as your application interacts with it, without having to modify any of the code or settings of your application.

Modularity is something to strive for, both in your application architecture, and in the structure of your code. Even if, for the moment, the only one taking advantage of that modularity is you in the context of your application, it's often a good idea to devote a few extra cycles to making your application fairly modular, so that either *you* can come along and change how things work without having to reinvent the wheel, or so that you can use that built-in modularity later, to enable better <u>configurability</u>.

DEFAULT FUNCTION PARAMETERS

As a rule (*to which there are virtually always exceptions, to be sure*), you should aim for at least **"functional-lite"** code, meaning that your functions should usually do one simple, specific thing. They should take some input and provide some output. In general (again, *most* of the time), when provided with the same input, your function should perform the same action, and provide an identical output. This applies regardless of what scope your function is running in, what scope it is called from, what other functions in the class are doing, or indeed whether the building the machine it's running on is on fire.

Even in the unending abyss that seals eternity at both ends,
if your function could compile to run on stray vacuum energy
and, given an input, it once returned some particular string,
it should, given that input, return that string again.
> [object Object]

Anyway, let's talk about what might be considered a sort of exception to this rule: **default function parameters**.

You could reasonably take either position; that this is, or is not, an exception to the "functional" rule. At least if well documented though, you can consider default function parameters to be just part of the effective "input" to a function. However, the question of whether it's "functional" or not is academic. It's a fine and useful thing to do. If anyone tells you different, just insult their mom[42] or something.

That'll show 'em.

Default function parameters are a type of **optional parameter**[43]. Optional parameters are, quite simply, parameters which can be left unspecified when calling your function, without causing any problems in its execution. For example, in the below function, the parameter `lastName` is optional. If specified, it will be used in the function. If not specified, it will not be used, but the function will still work perfectly well.

```
/**
 * @param {string} firstName - The greetee's first name.
 * @param {string} [lastName=] - The greetee's last name.
 * @return {string} - The greeting, as a string.
 */
function sayHi(firstName, lastName) {
    var greeting = 'Hello, ' + firstName;
    if (lastName) {
        greeting += ' ' + lastName;
    }
    greeting += '!';
    return greeting;
}
```

Fig. 10.04

---

[42] If you're stuck for context-appropriate "yo momma" jokes, you could try "Yo momma so FAT, she can only support addressable partitions up to 32GB in size".

I'm kidding. Please don't make fun of anyone's mother. Especially for their weight or appearance. Let's all just be kind to one another. <3

[43] Just a reminder: When **defining** a function, the variables you declare in the function header are called **"parameters"**. The values you pass into the function when calling it, are called **"arguments"**.

The **arguments** you pass into a function, are what determine the values of the function's **parameters** when it's run.

Note that the JSDoc[44] (the comments above the function beginning with /**) indicates that the parameter is optional, by wrapping it in square brackets and following the parameter name with an equals sign.

Since the `lastName` parameter has no default value, there's nothing after the equals sign. We could specify a default value for that parameter like so:

```
[lastName="Smith"]
```

Specifying a default value in the JSDoc isn't enough though, we need to also write a little code to detect that the parameter was not specified, and to set it to its default. For example, the following code checks if `lastName` is either not specified, or is a blank string (or some other falsey value such as `null`), and – if so – sets its value to the default:

```
/**
 * @param {string} firstName - The greetee's first name.
 * @param {string} [lastName="Smith"] - The greetee's last name.
 * @return {string} - The greeting, as a string.
 */
function sayHi(firstName, lastName) {
   var greeting;
   if (typeof lastName == 'undefined' || !lastName) {
      lastName = 'Smith';
   }
   greeting = 'Hello, ' + firstName + ' ' + lastName +
'!';
   return greeting;
}
```

Fig. 10.05

Since the value should now always be set to some value, we've also removed the condition that was on line 8, which checked whether `lastName` was set to a non-falsey value before appending it to the greeting.

Another way to specify a default value for a function parameter, is to use a **ternary**. Ternaries can seem somewhat arcane, and may make your code less readable. They should not necessarily be avoided, but should be used only when they can be made very simple; and they should never be "chained". In the following code, we've replaced the `if` block with a single ternary statement on **line 8**:

```
/**
 * @param {string} firstName - The greetee's first name.
 * @param {string} [lastName="Smith"] - The greetee's last name.
 * @return {string} - The greeting, as a string.
```

44 *For a refresher on JSDoc, see the* **Code comments** > **JSDoc** *section of the* **Code Documentation** *chapter of this book.*

132

```
*/
function sayHi(firstName, lastName) {
  var greeting;
  lastName = (typeof lastName == 'undefined') ? 'Smith' :
lastName;
  greeting = 'Hello, ' + firstName + ' ' + lastName +
'!';
  return greeting;
}
```

Fig. 10.06

Using default parameters in our functions can make them more modular, making it much easier to perform a single operation on different types of data. This can be very useful for keeping our code "**DRY**"[45]. We should, however, be careful to avoid writing *"everything-functions"*: functions which try to "do everything". It's up to your judgement to determine when to break some similar functionality out into one function, or two, or more.

RECORD SCRIPTS

One way to make your application more modular and customizable, is to off-load some of the control of its behavior to a collection of records in a table with a **Script** field. This is a special sort of field that, when displayed in the form, allows you to write JavaScript code, and provides basic JavaScript linting[46] functionality, syntax highlighting, and some other useful features like automatic indenting of nested code blocks.

The ability to write JavaScript code and store it in a record in a table in ServiceNow is cool but you may be asking yourself, "what does that actually... do?" – Well, think about it; Business Rules are basically just scripts stored in a table (`sys_script`), right? Something must tell that script to execute, and how. Turns out, we can do the same thing!

This will all probably become much clearer with an example, so let's consider a scenario in which we have an application which exports records from the Incident table in ServiceNow, and sends them off to some other system. Maybe the other system is an archive, or maybe they're doing some external analysis on the data – doesn't matter. We need to get the data out of ServiceNow, and into this other system.

That may seem straightforward. Just write a Script Include with some methods to do the work of packaging up an Incident into a JSON object. Make

---

[45] *As a reminder: DRY stands for "Don't Repeat Yourself". DRY code avoids repeating a code block over and over, to accomplish a nearly identical goal.*

[46] *"Linting" means using a tool to analyze your code to flag bugs, errors, syntactical issues, etc. (such as missing semicolons or malformed code blocks).*

sure it's structured in whatever way the receiving system wants it to be structured. Maybe write a Business Rule or Scheduled Script Execution to trigger the export trigger (depending on whether we want the data exported immediately upon update, or once every so-often, respectively).

Remember though, we're trying to make our application as **modular** and **configurable** as possible.

What if the receiving system is another ticketing platform, and it calculates priority differently than ServiceNow does? If that's the case, you'll have to do some calculation to determine what the appropriate priority in the new system *ought* to be, based on data in the ticket in ServiceNow.

"Okay, no problem." you might say, *"I'll just write a special handler function for calculating the Priority value that we send to the target system"*.

Then you learn that the target system has a maximum character count in the description field, of only 1,000 characters; and worse, that passing in too many characters causes a hard failure resulting in the record being rejected.

"Okay", you continue. *"I can write a special handler for that as well"*.

And the **State** field in the target system is of course, not an integer, like it is in ServiceNow.

"Third special handler; no biggie", you say, as you die a little inside.

Oh, and did they forget to mention? The target system only has one layer of category – no subcategory field – and the categories and subcategories don't match up with what's in ServiceNow.

"Uh... I guess I could write a sort of a nested hash-map that—"

And they want to be able to easily map custom fields from ServiceNow, as they're added, without having to sort through what is now a *massive* Script Include to slip the code in-between all your special handlers.

"Er..."

Wouldn't it be nice if there were a better way[47]?

Oh good, there is: scripted control records.

Let's dive into an example of how one might handle this scenario. I'm going to skip some of the basics when it doesn't matter, just for the sake of this example.

---

[47] *This is where I would have put a meme of Billy Mays saying, "There's got to be a better way!", but I'm pretty sure I'd get dinged for some kind of obscure copyright thing.*

DEFINING SCRIPTED RECORDS

We're going to create the scripted records first, which might be a little confusing until we get to the part where we invoke the scripts in those records, but stay with me; I promise it'll make sense by the end.

First, let's create a table to store some records that will comprise the "field mappings" from the Incident table to whatever table the records are going into, in the target system. Let's call that table `inc_export_map`[48].

After saving the table record, let's add a couple of fields:

1. Active [active]
   a. **Type**: True/False
   b. **Default value**: true
2. Source field name [source_field_name]
   a. **Type**: String
   b. **Max length**: 40
   c. **Mandatory**: true
3. Target field name [target_field_name]
   a. **Type**: String
   b. **Max length**: 40
   c. **Mandatory**: true
   d. **Display**: true
   e. **Unique**: true
4. Use transform [use_transform]
   a. **Type**: True/False
   b. **Default value**: false
5. Transform script [transform_script]
   a. **Type**: Script
   b. **Max length**: 40000

When finished, our table should look something like this, and then we can hit **Save**:

---

[48] *Don't forget what we learned in the **Naming Conventions** chapter: table names are always singular!*

	Column label	Column name ▲	Type	Reference	Max length	Default value	Display	Mandatory
ⓘ	Created by	sys_created_by	String	(empty)	40		false	false
ⓘ	Created	sys_created_on	Date/Time	(empty)	40		false	false
ⓘ	Sys ID	sys_id	Sys ID (GUID)	(empty)	32		false	false
ⓘ	Updates	sys_mod_count	Integer	(empty)	40		false	false
ⓘ	Updated by	sys_updated_by	String	(empty)	40		false	false
ⓘ	Updated	sys_updated_on	Date/Time	(empty)	40		false	false
✕	Active	active	True/False			true	false	false
✕	Source field name	source_field_name	String	40			false	true
✕	Target field name	target_field_name	String	40			true	true
✕	Use tranform	use_tranform	True/False			false	false	false
✕	Transform script	transform_script	Script	4000	answer = ''; //Set the answer variable t...	false	false
+	Insert a new row...							

Now, just to help ourselves and our users out, let's add a **default value** for the **Transform script** field, that gives the user a bit of scaffolding. We could have the script evaluate to set a variable that we define, such as answer, by using something simple like this:

```
answer = ''; //Set answer to the target field value.
```

Then, in the code we use to invoke the script in this field, we would simply need to retrieve the final value of that variable after the script's execution (for which there is a simple API in ServiceNow that we'll see later).

However, we're going to want to pass in a couple of other variables so that they can be used *within* the script, which requires a slightly more complex bit of scaffolding. Let's take Business Rules as an example. – In a Business Rule, there is a function which has passed into it, two important variables: current, and previous. As a reminder, here is the default value for an advanced Business Rule's script field:

```
(function executeRule(current, previous /*null when
async*/) {

    // Add your code here

})(current, previous);
```

Fig. 10.07

As you can see, the executeRule function is defined on line 1, and is in what's called an "IIFE", which stands for **Immediately Invoked Function Expression**. What makes this function "immediately invoked", is the () on the last line, into which are passed the current and previous variables. This is just a method for declaring and invoking a function in a **single statement**. This pattern functions basically exactly the same as if you were to *declare* a function and *then* execute it using two separate statements, like so:

```
function executeRule(current, previous /*null when
async*/) {
    // Add your code here
}

executeRule(current, previous);
```
Fig. 10.08

The `current` and `previous` variables are defined as **arguments** in the function header on line 1, but they aren't defined outside the function; so how can they be *passed in* to the function as **arguments**? Well, as we'll see shortly, these variables are defined by the script that *invokes* the code in this record. There is an API for executing scripts inside of records like this (`GlideScopedEvaluator`), and it handles that part for us.

Before we get to talking about how to invoke our script though, let's write our script field's default value. Using the pattern that Business Rules use as an example, we're going to set our script's default value to something like this:

```
(function doTransform(current, sourceFieldName,
sourceFieldValue, targetFieldName) {

    var targetFieldValue = sourceFieldValue.toString();
    //Add your code here, and return the target field
value.
    return targetFieldValue;

})(current, sourceFieldName, sourceFieldValue,
targetFieldName);
```
Fig. 10.09

In this script, we're passing in four variables: `current` (the current record for which we're doing the transformation), `sourceFieldName` (the name of the source field, based on the current transform record), `sourceFieldValue` (the original value of the source field in ServiceNow), and `targetFieldName` (the target field name, based on the current transform record). In the transform script, we can use any (or none) of those variables to do our transformation, and then return the final target field value.

Now that we've got a decent default value for our script field, we'll go to that field's dictionary record, and set the **Default value** field to our script. It won't be syntax-highlighted in the field, but that's okay – it will be on the transform record.

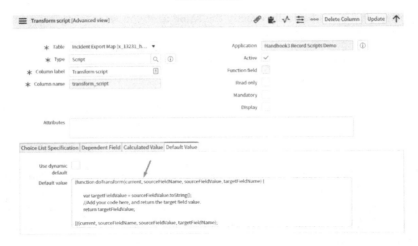

If this were a "real" application, this is the part where we'd go in and fiddle with the form layout to make it pretty, and then add a UI Policy to make it so the **Transform script** field only shows up when **Use transform** is set to true, but this is just an example so I'm going to skip those steps.

One thing to know about these script fields, is that there are two main ways to get data *out* of them, after running them (which, again, we'll see how to do shortly). As mentioned above, you can choose a variable (such as `answer`), have the script set the value of that variable to whatever you want the result to be, then *retrieve* the value of that variable after the script has executed. Note that this would **not** work with the pattern that we're using, because our `targetFieldValue` variable is wrapped in a function scope. However, if we were to remove the function wrapper, then we *could* just set that variable to the desired value and retrieve it using our calling script; but then we wouldn't be able to explicitly pass in the variables we're making available to the script (like `current` and `sourceFieldValue`). Even though those variables would still technically be available within the script, it would be more confusing and harder to know what exactly you had available to you while writing the transform script.

The second way of getting some value out of our transform script, is to simply have it **evaluate to** the final target field value. The idea of a script **evaluating to** some value might be a new one, so here's a quick lesson:

To simplify quite a bit, a script "evaluates to" whatever the **final expression** evaluates to. Consider the following script:

```
var myName = 'Tim';
var greeting = 'Hello, ' + myName;
```
Fig. 10.10

This script does not actually evaluate to *anything*, because although the last statement in the script is doing work, that statement does not return a value; therefore, it does not "evaluate to" anything. You can test this yourself, by opening up your web browser (preferably Chrome), pressing **F12**, navigating to the **Console**, and entering this code there. Upon pressing **Enter**, you'll probably see a line show up that says something like `undefined`. That's because your script didn't evaluate to anything!

```
> var myName = 'Tim';
  var greeting = 'Hello, ' + myName;
<· undefined ◄———
```

If we add a third line, however, we can cause our little script to evaluate to the value of `greeting`:

```
var myName = 'Tim';
var greeting = 'Hello, ' + myName;
greeting;
```
Fig. 10.11

That third line "evaluates to" the value of `greeting`, which – since it's the last statement in our script – means that *our script evaluates to* the value of `greeting`!

```
> var myName = 'Tim';
  var greeting = 'Hello, ' + myName;
  greeting;
<· "Hello, Tim" ◄
```

Now, applying this lesson to our scripted records, you might be able to see how our script evaluates to whatever value the function returns. The function, being an IIFE, is immediately invoked (or *run*), and since the combination declaration-and-invocation of that function is the *last statement* in our script, that means that *our script evaluates to* whatever that function returns!

Pro-tip: If we were to add another line of code below our function – even something like `var a = 3;` *– it would mean that our script would no longer evaluate to the value returned by the function!*

INVOKING SCRIPTED RECORDS

Now that we've got our **Incident Export Map** table defined, and our **Transform script** field is set up with a useful default value, it's time to write the code that will actually *use* these potentially-scripted records, invoking the scripts within them and using the values they return.

First, we need to get an Incident record to do the transformation on. Once we have that, we need to loop through all our active export map records for that Incident and evaluate each of them. We'll focus on the function responsible for doing the actual transformation.

The API class we're going to be making use of to execute these scripts, is called `GlideScopedEvaluator`[49]. This class has the methods `.putVariable()`, `.getVariable()`, and `.evaluateScript()`. It's the `.evaluateScript()` method that we're going to use, since it has optional parameters allowing us to specify the variables to pass into the script in the export map's script field, so we don't need to use the `.putVariable()` method (although we could, if we wanted).

Now comes the big chunk of code that ties everything we've done so far together. Read through it yourself once and see if you can identify what all it's doing, then I'll walk you through the code line-by-line, below.

```
function getTransformedFieldVals(grIncident) {
    var sourceFieldName, targetFieldName, sourceFieldVal;
    var mappedValues = {};
    var gsEval = new GlideScopedEvaluator();
    var grExportMap = new GlideRecord(
        'x_13231_hb3_rec_sc_inc_export_map'
    );
    grExportMap.addActiveQuery();
    grExportMap.query();
    while (grExportMap.next()) {
        sourceFieldName =
grExportMap.getValue('source_field_name');
        targetFieldName =
grExportMap.getValue('target_field_name');
        sourceFieldVal =
grIncident.getValue(sourceFieldName);
        //If scripted transform isn't necessary, just set
        // target value from source value & continue.
        if (grExportMap.getValue('use_transform') != '1') {
            mappedValues[targetFieldName] = sourceFieldVal;
            continue; //Continue to next loop iteration.
        }
```

---

[49] *API docs for* `GlideScopedEvaluator` *can be found here:*

https://developer.servicenow.com/dev.do#!/reference/api/quebec/server/no-namespace/c_GlideEvaluatorScopedAPI

```
        mappedValues[targetFieldName] =
gsEval.evaluateScript(
            grExportMap, //GR for map record
            'transform_script', //Script field,
            { //Variables to be accessible within the
script
                'current': grIncident,
                'sourceFieldName': sourceFieldName,
                'sourceFieldValue': sourceFieldVal,
                'targetFieldName': targetFieldName
            }
        );
    }
    return mappedValues;
}
```

Fig. 10.12: Getting all transformed field values for a provided Incident.

Let's go line-by-line, and analyze what's happening here.

Line 2: "Hoisted" variable declarations, to keep our code clean and to make sure our code is *written* as close to how the JavaScript engine will actually *run* it as possible.

Ln 3-7: Declaring a variable containing an empty object (which is where our transformed field values will end up), our instantiation of GlideScopedEvaluator (which we'll use to evaluate the scripts in our export map records), and a GlideRecord object we'll use to query the Export Map table.

Ln 8-10: Querying the Export Map table; getting only **active** export map records.

Ln 11-13: Getting the values that we'll use to determine the target field value (whether by running a transform script or just getting the original field value).

Ln 16-19: Checking if the **Use transform** field is **not** set to true. If it isn't set to true, then just set the mapped value to the original value from ServiceNow, and continue; - meaning stop the current iteration of the while loop, and skip on to the next one.

Ln 20-29: Call the .evaluateScript() method of gsEval (our instance of the GlideScopedEvaluator class). For the first argument, we're passing in the GlideRecord corresponding to the specific export map record we're working on. The second argument is the name of the script field within that record. The third and final argument is an object containing a list of key:value pairs, where the *key* is the name of a variable to be available within the script as it runs, and the *value* is the actual value of that variable when the script executes. The .evaluateScript() method **returns** whatever value the script in the script field evaluates to, so we're adding the evaluated value to the mappedValues object.

Ln 31: Finally, once we've looped through all export map records and finished adding all mapped fields and mapped (or transformed) values to the `mappedValues` object, return that object, which should now contain a complete representation of the record in the target system, including all mapped fields and values.

The beauty of this approach is that in order to add new fields to the mapping, we don't need to add code! We simply need to add a new export map record! We *can* write some code in the export map record, but if no transformation is necessary, we can just leave the **Use transform** field unchecked, and the original value from the source field in ServiceNow will be sent along for the target field.

SECURITY

It's not just hackers you have to worry about

"I wonder what happens if I select everything in this table and click the 'Delete' button..."
—*Your users*

"The greatest threat to any computer system, is its users."
—*Tim Woodruff, I guess*

THE SECURITY OF AN INSTANCE is just as important as anything else. Whether you're an architect, a developer, or an admin, you are at least partially responsible for maintaining the security of the instance, just as you are for maintaining its integrity and performance.

This chapter will cover a few guidelines, best-practices, and tips that your fearless author and other industry veterans have picked up to keep things safe and secure.

ACLS (SECURITY RULES)

Security rules (ACLs) are the primary means by which role-based permissions are granted.

There are three types of ACLs. In order of specificity, they are:

1. Table-level
2. Record/row-level
3. Field-level

They work as you might expect: Table-level ACLs grant access to a table. Record-level ACLs grant access to the records within a table, and field-level ACLs grant access to specific fields within a table.

One thing to keep in mind when dealing with ACLs, is that they are **permissive**; not restrictive. If there is an ACL which grants you access to something, you'll have it. If there is not an ACL which grants access to that thing, then you won't have it. There is no need to create a "restrictive" ACL, and in fact that would not accomplish anything. If a person already has permissive access to an object (such as a table, record, or field) then creating another ACL which they do not meet the criteria for does not block their access to that object. Remember though, that this only applies to creating multiple ACLs on the **same object**.

The more **specific** the ACL, the higher its priority. Because of this, you **can** override (or "**mask**") another ACL. For example, if you have an ACL which grants access to a base table like the **Task** [task] table, and you create a new ACL of the same type on the **Incident** [incident] table, you can expect that it would **override** the Task rule. By the same token, if you create an ACL on the **short description** field of the Incident table (**incident.short_description**), you can expect that it would override an "**incident.***" rule which uses the wildcard "*****" to indicate that it applies to all fields on the incident table.

If you're ever unsure about the execution plan for a given ACL, you can use the **Show ACL Execution Plan** UI Action at the bottom of the ACL form:

Related Links

Show ACL Execution Plan

This will open a dialog which displays the execution plan of the specific ACL you're looking at, with respect to other ACLs for the same object and the same operation. Clicking **Show all** at the bottom of this dialog will allow you to see any ACLs that the current rule is **masking** or overriding.

Since the **admin** role (discussed in the next section) can **override** many ACLs, it's important to carefully consider whether the **admin overrides** checkbox on a given ACL is enabled. If you have personally identifiable information (PII) or sensitive restricted data in your instance, such as certain data you might find inside of HR records, you should consider creating a separate ACL that's dependent on a separate role. In this case, you would want to be sure to **disable** the "admin overrides" checkbox on the ACL that grants access to this sensitive data.

QUERY BUSINESS RULES

Query Business Rules (QBRs) are an interesting alternative to (or better yet, *addition to* ACLs). They execute right as the query is initiated, but before it's sent to the database server. Their primary use is to refine a query and add additional query parameters.

QBRs have some down-sides (such as making it much more difficult to troubleshoot access and visibility issues), but they also have some great situational advantages. Two main advantages are:

Privacy: When querying a table from the list view, ACLs result in a message indicating how many rows were removed due to security rules. QBRs do not. This comes in especially handy when you're dealing with HR tickets, or tickets which may be subject to extra privacy regulations (such as HIPAA). Consider an example in which a sneaky user wants to know if anyone has submitted an HR case against them. Well, of course you'd have ACLs ensuring that only HR case managers or the **requestor** of a case can see it; you wouldn't want the **subject person** (the one about whom the HR case is) to necessarily see reports against them. However, if Sneaky McSneakerson over there queries the HR Case table for cases where he is the subject person but not the requestor, even though they can't see the cases, they *will* be able to see how many there are, because of the message at the bottom of the list, indicating how many records were hidden due to security constraints! This user can then further refine his query to try to find out who it was that was submitting cases against them.

Performance: Unfortunately, ACLs (and ACL scripts) execute against **every single record** returned from a query. Obviously if your query returns 10,000 records, this can be detrimental from a performance perspective, as the ACL script must run 10,000 times! QBRs only run once, before the query even executes, and refine the query to reduce the total number of records returned from the database. This also means that your ACLs need to execute against fewer records, since QBRs run first, and ACLs only run against records *returned* from the database.

The down-side to QBRs, is that they're more difficult to troubleshoot, and can be confusing. Users may be confused as to why some records aren't showing up when the query shown in the list UI doesn't look like it should exclude those records, since QBRs don't add query parameters to the query builder.

They can also cause confusion for developers, if not written *very carefully*. This is in part, because of a weird quirk in SQL standards whereby if you add a query like *some_field != some_value*, it will **not only** exclude records where that field is not equal to that value, but it will also **exclude any records where that field is blank!**[50] – Crazy, right? But that's not a quirk of ServiceNow, it is apparently part of the SQL standard.

Is it appropriate to use an eyeroll emoji in a book about software development? ☐

Imagine you have a table with the following records:

Shoes

Number	Material	Description
01	Suede	Blue suede shoes
02	Leather	Leather loafers
03	Silk	Silk sandals

---

[50] *You can read more about QBRs, as well as about this weird behavior of SQL and how to get around it in my article on the topic, at http://qbr.snc.guru/.*

| 04 | | Barefoot |
| 05 | Metal | Metal moccasins |

Most of the records have a value in the Material field, but Barefoot [04] doesn't. This is perfectly fine, as Material is not a required field.

Now, let's introduce a Query Business Rule that contains the following code:

```
//Only allow admins to see my blue suede shoes
if (!gs.hasRole('admin')) {
    current.addQuery('material', '!=', 'Suede');
}
```

Fig. 11.01

This query results in the following records being returned for anyone who isn't an admin:

Number	Material	Description
02	Leather	Leather loafers
03	Silk	Silk Sandals
05	Metal	Metal moccasins

Now, anyone who isn't an admin will not be able to see my Blue Suede Shoes in that table. -- But wait, what's this? Where is Barefoot [04]?

A blank string "" is not equal to the string "Suede"; not even loosely equal. If we're worried we might be going insane, we can even test this by running the following line of code in our browser console:

```
console.log('' != 'Suede');
```

(which of course, prints `true`).

But SQL doesn't care about your *foolish human logic*, because adding a "**not equal to**" query on any string field, filters out all blank values! Why? I assume because SQL hates you is why. I was unable to find any other explanation for this behavior.

Let's say you've thought about it carefully, and a query Business Rule really is the best solution for what you're trying to do. How do you get around this SQL weirdness, so you can add a "*not equal to*" query, using a query Business Rule? Well as it happens, you can do so in the same way that the platform does for you automatically (sometimes)!

If you have a table of shoes just like the one in the above example, and you use the query builder to do an "is not" query, you run into the same issue where records where that field is blank don't show up.

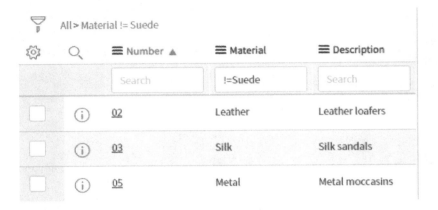

BUT – if, instead of using the query builder, you **right-clicked** on "**Suede**" in the **Material** column, and clicked on **Filter out**, you would get the results you'd expect:

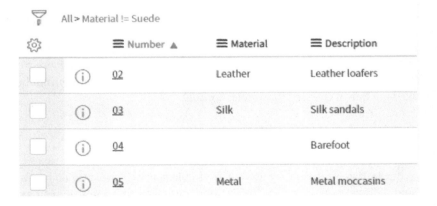

It works! — but *why*? **What is this sorcery!?**

What's going on is that even though the UI shows you a neat little breadcrumb that just says "**Material != Suede**", the platform *pulled a sneaky on ya*[51]! If you expand the filter builder, you'll see that the actual query says "**Material is not Suede** *or* **Material is NULL**".

---

[51] https://youtu.be/pg0_a2_7a1c

Taking a hint from this behavior, we can resolve the issue whenever we want to add an **"is not"** query (or ***"is different from"***, or ***"same as"***, *since those have the same issues*) through a query Business Rule or even through the query builder on a list, by also adding an "or condition" that says "**or [*field name*] is [*'NULL'*]**" – and yes, actually passing in the string "*NULL*". See the following Business Rule script for an example:

```
(function executeRule(current, previous /*null when
async*/) {
    current.addQuery('u_material', '!=',
'Suede').addOrCondition('u_material', 'NULL');
})(current, previous);
```
Fig. 11.02

This issue (and solution) are not actually specific to query Business Rules – This is regular old everyday SQL behavior. If you have a filter that says "[***some field***] is not [*some value*]" and you want blank values to show up in the results, you must add "**...or [*that field*] is '*NULL*'**".

Note: *You could also use "...is" followed by a blank string, or "...is empty" (instead of "...is 'NULL'"), but it's worth mentioning that only "...is 'NULL'" hides the sub-condition to make the query breadcrumb look nice and succinct. This doesn't matter for QBRs though, as their conditions don't show up in the condition builder.*

THE ADMIN ROLE

The **admin** role is the role which allows users to do *pretty much* anything they want. The only exception is certain security operations like modifying ACLs, which requires the **security_admin** role.

Note: *If you have the **High security settings** plugin enabled, in earlier versions of ServiceNow like Fuji and Geneva, the **security_admin** role is also required in order to run background scripts.*

The **admin** role grants access to scripts and other administrative tools within the platform, but it also allows you to override most ACLs (security rules). If you have the admin role, you will likely not even realize when you are overriding an ACL. This can lead to some bad situations.

Consider a scenario in which you are asked to update a Change record; however, your organization has an integration which expects certain modifications not to be made to change records under certain circumstances. If this is enforced by an ACL with the **Admin overrides** check-box set to **true**, the system will allow you to make that change. What's worse, it would not even inform you that you've just overridden an ACL to do so! For this reason, if you might ever need to do things like update tickets in production, it's a good idea to set up a separate **admin** account, and use your "normal" account for any tasks such as updating tickets and performing normal "non-admin" tasks.

It is important to be judicious when assigning the admin role to people in your environment. If someone requires a specific role for testing, ensure that they only get that role in the sub-prod environment in which they'll be testing. It's also a good idea to ensure that there are procedures in place to make sure that those roles are revoked once they are no longer needed.

*Pro-tip: I've written a tool specifically for granting **temporary** permissions to a **user** or **group**. These roles expire according to a schedule that you can set. You can find this completely free tool at: http://temppermissions.snc.guru/.*

If you typically use a single account for your "admin" duties, as well as for creating and updating tasks, approving changes, and so on, it would be easy to **accidentally** utilize your "admin override" functionality *without even knowing it*. There is no notification or other indicator when you're only able to see some option because you're an admin and thus overriding an ACL! You might end up accidentally making some change that you shouldn't be able to make, such as approving or changing the state of a change record that would otherwise be locked down.

To avoid this, some companies require that admins have two separate accounts: one "normal" account with their group's non-admin roles, and a separate "admin" account that they must log into locally on the instance. This is an okay solution, but requires a lot of flipping back-and-forth, makes it difficult to update tickets as you're working on stuff, and often leads to people just using their admin account for everything because it's more convenient.

There is potentially, a better way. To avoid accidentally using your "admin powers" when you don't mean to, you can simply configure the **admin** role to be an **elevated privilege**.

Okay, so perhaps "simply" wasn't the right word to use there, but it can be done without too much hassle. Unfortunately, the **Elevate privilege** field on the admin role is protected by an ACL that cannot be modified or deactivated based on its protection policy. While you cannot bypass the protection policy to modify this ACL, you *can* bypass the ACL itself using a background script (since **scripted GlideRecord operations typically ignore ACLs** – which is an important fact to be aware of!). To make **admin** an elevated privilege, follow the steps below:

1. Elevate to **Security admin** so you can modify role records.
2. Open the **background scripts** module from **System Definition > Scripts – Background**.
3. Run the following script:

```
var grAdminRole = new GlideRecord('sys_user_role');
grAdminRole.addQuery('name', 'admin');
grAdminRole.setLimit(1);
grAdminRole.query();
if (grAdminRole.next()) {
    grAdminRole.setValue('elevated_privilege', true);
    grAdminRole.update();
}
```

Fig. 11.03

4. Navigate to the **admin** role in the **sys_user_role** table, and update the description to something more succinct (since this will show in the "elevate roles" dialog).

Elevate Roles

The following are session-specific privileges, session timeout or logout will remove all elevated privileges.

☐ admin

The System Administrator role. Elevate to this role to perform administrative tasks.

☐ security_admin

Grant modification access to High Security Settings, allow user to modify the Access Control List

More Info   Cancel   OK

You should be aware however, that this has risks. Making the admin role an elevated privilege, means that any system accounts which rely on the admin role, or accounts used for administrative privileges such as pulling update sets from a sub-prod instance, will need to have additional roles manually added to them, to ensure that they can do what they need to, even without being able to elevate to the admin role manually.

I have found this to be worth the inconvenience of adding additional roles where appropriate, but as with virtually every significant change, you should have a test-run of this in your environment, before implementing it widely.

GLIDERECORD VS. GLIDERECORDSECURE

ACLs are the primary means by which table-security is applied in ServiceNow. ACLs can secure different table operations (read, write, delete, etc.) based on a given **role, condition**, and/or the evaluation of a given **script** in the ACL.

Scripted **GlideRecord** operations, such as the one mentioned in the section on the *admin* role for making it into an elevated privilege, usually **ignore ACL-based security** in ServiceNow. This is an important point to consider when building virtually any scripts, for a few reasons which might not be immediately apparent.

One up-side to the behavior of **GlideRecord**, is that it allows your scripts to read, and even modify, records that the user for whom the script is being executed may not have access to. This makes your life as a developer much easier in a lot of cases. For example, let's say you've got a user who has access to view and modify records in the **Incident** table, but not the **HR Case** table. You may want this user to be able to click a Form UI Action on an Incident record that creates an HR case, copying some details from the Incident to the case in the process. However, you don't want to grant the user access to view or create tickets in the HR case table directly. This can be accomplished easily, by simply using a **GlideRecord** script to create the HR case, in the UI Action script. The following script will work just fine, whether the user who clicks the UI Action has permissions to create the target record, or not.

```
createHRCase(current);

function createHRCase(current) {
    var hrFieldName, hrFieldValue, hrCaseID, hrCaseNumber;
    /**
     * Key: field name on the sn_hr_core_case table.
     * Value: Value to put into the field in the key.
     * @type {{}}
     */
    var fieldMap = {
        'hr_service' : '607e03320b30220097432da0d5673a23',
//Some generic HR service
        'short_description' :
current.getValue('short_description'),
        'description' : 'Transferred from Incident ' +
            current.getValue('number') + '\n' +
current.getValue('description'),
        'skills' : 'b0370019f22120047a2d126c42e706f',
//"HR"
        'parent' : current.getUniqueValue()
    };
    var grHRCase = new GlideRecord('sn_hr_core_case');

    grHRCase.initialize();
    for (hrFieldName in fieldMap) {
        if (!fieldMap.hasOwnProperty(hrFieldName)) {
            //Avoid iterating into inherited/prototype
properties
            continue;
        }
        hrFieldValue = fieldMap[hrFieldName];
        grHRCase.setValue(hrFieldName, hrFieldValue);
    }
    grHRCase.insert(); //Ignores ACLs
```

```
    gs.addInfoMessage('HR case ' +
grHRCase.getValue('number') + ' created.');
    }
```

Fig. 10.04

The script would be able to create the case, even though the user who clicked the UI Action to trigger it doesn't have access to view or create records in that table!

On the other hand, there are times when you want to perform a scripted operation as a result of a user action, but **only** if the user has permissions to perform that operation. For example, imagine the above scenario, except you only want the agent to be able to create an HR case if they have access to create HR cases in the first place.

One common way to do this, might be to use the GlideRecord `.canCreate()`, `.canRead()`, and `.canWrite()` methods. However, to simplify the process of checking whether the user can read, write, or create a record, you may want to simply use the GlideRecordSecure class.

The **GlideRecordSecure** class is an extension of GlideRecord which performs all the same functions as the GlideRecord class, but also ensures that the operation being performed (read, write, etc.) is allowed by the security rules on the table. Any records which are not visible to the user for whom the script is being executed, will simply not be iterated into when using GlideRecordSecure's `.next()` method. Any fields which the user cannot write to, will not be updated. Any fields which cannot be read, will show up as *NULL*. Calling `.isValidField()` on a field which the user doesn't have read access to read from, will return *false*.

Keep in mind that GlideRecordSecure does cause ACLs to be evaluated which has performance implications, so it should not be used as a complete replacement for GlideRecord in all circumstances.

SERVICE PORTAL

Ooh, shiny

You can spread jelly on peanut butter, but you can't spread peanut butter on jelly.
—Dick Van Dyke

THE SERVICE PORTAL is one of the newer introductions to the ServiceNow platform, having been introduced in the Helsinki version. At its release, it broke a lot of functionality, prevented a lot of client scripts and catalog client scripts from running properly, and generally made a mess of things. However, it was generally accepted as a suitable replacement for the old Jelly-based "CMS" UI, largely because Jelly is the worst pseudo-language to have ever been invented.

Although the Service Portal came with a lot of annoyances, many of them have since been resolved and it is now a powerful and functional tool to have in your arsenal, for presenting information and forms to your end-users.

It is not within the scope of this book to teach you the basics of service portal development (for that, see my other book: **Learning ServiceNow - Second Edition**: http://lsn.snc.guru/). However, in this chapter, we'll learn some important pro-tips for portal development, as well as some pitfalls to avoid!

CLIENT SCRIPTS

Whether it's client scripts or catalog client scripts, by **default**, they will not run in the service portal. This is because of a field on client scripts called **UI Type**. This field has three options: **Desktop**, **Mobile / Service Portal**, and **All**. UI policies and catalog UI policies with scripts (which execute just like client scripts) have a similar field, called **Run scripts in UI type**. This field has the same options as the client script **UI Type** field. However, it should be noted that on UI policies, this field only affects whether the **script** portion of the UI policy runs on the service portal or mobile UI. The **UI policy actions** run either way.

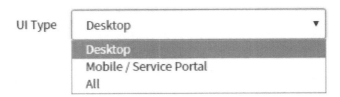

The default value for both of these types of fields, is **Desktop**. When "Desktop" is selected however, the script **will not execute in the service portal**... even when viewed from a <u>desktop</u>. If that sounds dumb to you, you're not alone. However, selecting "All" for this field will cause the script to execute in both UIs.

Pro-tip: *I highly recommend changing the default value of all of these fields to "**All**". Otherwise, if you forget to update this field, your scripts won't run on the portal by default.*

This is not an arbitrary choice, since many APIs and a big chunk of other functionality will not run in the Service Portal. The majority of these limitations can be summed up as:

1. No direct Document Object Model (DOM) access or manipulation
    a. This includes both direct access to the document object, as well as DOM access using built-in client-side ServiceNow APIs such as `gel()`, `g_form.getElement()`, and `g_form.getControl()`.
2. No synchronous server-client communication (such as the GlideRecord `.query()` or GlideElement `.getReference()` methods without a callback function, the GlideRecord `.get()` method entirely, or the synchronous GlideAjax `.getXMLWait()` method).

a. Unfortunately, this prevents you from being able to have an onSubmit script wait for a query or GlideAjax operation to complete before allowing or preventing form submission, so you have to get a bit clever about how you handle that – but it's doable.

b. I've written a detailed article about asynchronicity, GlideAjax, and callback functions in general, at: http://ajax.snc.guru/.

These limitations obviously may cause a few problems, especially when doing things like checking that a catalog item has an attachment before allowing submission (which could only be done using DOM manipulation in the past).

In order to resolve some of these issues, I've written a tool that re-enables access to the above APIs, and to the DOM. It is free to use at your own risk. You can find the article and free tool, at http://attachments.snc.guru/. This tool not only exposes methods for requiring attachments upon submission in a new, custom sp_form object, but it also provides methods for directly accessing variable form elements. It should be noted however, that if ServiceNow decides to change how it identifies variable elements in a catalog item form on the service portal, this tool will no longer work for that purpose (but should still work for requiring attachments).

It is also not as simple as switching all of your client and catalog client scripts' UI types from "Desktop" to "All". Since there are different sets of functionality and APIs available on the service portal UI versus everywhere else on the platform, and since you can't just ignore the behavior in the rest of the platform, you've got to decide how to make your scripts work in **both**. This can be done in a couple of ways:

1. Use two scripts. This means creating two versions of your entire script: One with the **UI type** field set to **Desktop**, and the other set to **Mobile / Service Portal**. This does not result in performance degradation, since only one type of script will be loaded from the server at a time, depending on what type of page is being loaded. However, it does create two separate places where your code must be maintained for one piece of functionality.

2. Use one script, and a condition to check if you're in the portal. This is the method I recommend and prefer, so this is what I'll discuss below.

To use option two, set your script's **UI Type** field to **All**, and have the two different versions of your code execute based on the results of a condition like so:

```
var inPortal = !document;
```

```
if (inPortal) {
    doSomethingPortal();
} else {
    doSomethingCMS();
}
//Define functions below...
```
Fig. 12.01

WIDGETS & THE CATALOG

Occasionally in the "old" CMS UI, you would need to have a complex element embedded into your catalog item form. In these cases, you would often use a UI Macro (written in Jelly, unfortunately). However, **UI macros are not supported in the portal** and they will not render (although anything in the **Instructions** field on a **Macro** variable, *will* still show up). There is an easy way around this however, without even having to break your existing CMS functionality.

On a catalog variable record with the **Type** field set to **Macro**, you'll see the typical **Macro** and **Summary macro** fields which should point to your UI macro. However, if you move over to the **Default Value** form section, you'll see a **Widget** field. I have no idea why it's in the Default Value section, but just go with it. In this field, you can specify a portal widget (from the *sp_widget* table) to be displayed instead of the UI macro whenever the catalog item is rendered in the service portal.

You can access the value of other variables on the form from within your widget, using $scope.page.g_form.getValue('variable_name');.

***Pro-tip:** If you need to execute some logic or alter the behavior of a widget based on a change to the value of some variable or field rather than based on a click, you can do so by using the $rootScope object. For example:*

```
$rootScope.$on("field.change", function(evt, parms) {
    if (parms.field.variable_name = 'variable_name') {
        //Do something here.
        //Access the new value with parms.newValue
    }
});
```

Fig. 12.02

THE PORTAL RECORD

Since you can render pretty much any portal page in any portal, you may occasionally need to access some information about the specific portal your code is being rendered on. For example, you might want some bit to appear differently based on which **theme** the portal you're on is using.

You can access information about the portal record from the *sp_portal* table in your code, by using `$sp.getValue()`. For example, you can determine which theme the portal your code has loaded on is using, with: `$sp.getValue('theme')`. You can see an example of this in out-of-box code, by looking at the SC Categories widget, which uses `$sp.getValue('sc_catalog')`, in order to get the catalog in the "catalog" field of the current portal record. This is so you can use different catalogs with different portals without messing with the page/widget structure.

WIDGETS: INSTANCES & OPTIONS

A **widget** is a record which contains a definition of some content which would be rendered on a service portal page. The widget itself, is agnostic of what page – or even what portal it is rendered in.

A **widget instance** is a record that's created for each instance of a particular widget added to a page. If you add one widget to the same page twice, you have two **widget instances** on that page, both of which would be **instances** of the same **widget** record.

Note: *It's actually possible to create a widget instance without associating it to a particular page. That instance can then be called from the server script of another widget, using* $sp.getWidgetFromInstance('instance_id_name')$.

A widget's **option schema** consists of customizable values that can control how a widget looks or behaves between different widget instances. Option schema is a powerful feature that allows a single widget to do multiple related jobs. For example, you might have three instances of a single clock widget on your page, each configured to display the time in a different time-zone. The specific time-zone in that case, could be specified via the clock widget's option schema.

While you can view and modify a widget's **option schema** from the **Widget** record itself, it's actually much easier and more intuitive to edit it from the **Widget Editor**! To get there, open up the Widget record (*not* the widget *instance*), and click **Open in Widget Editor** under **Related Links**. Once there, click on the hamburger menu at the top-right of the editor, and click **Edit option schema**.

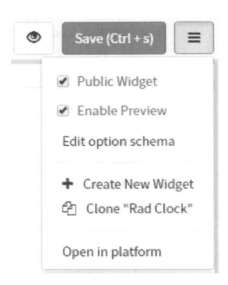

In the corresponding dialog, you'll see several fields for each option: **Label**, **Name**, **Type**, **Hint**, **Default value**, and **Form section**. Only **Label**, **Name**, **Type**, and **Form section** are mandatory. Each **option** in an **option schema** will have a corresponding value for each of these mandatory fields.

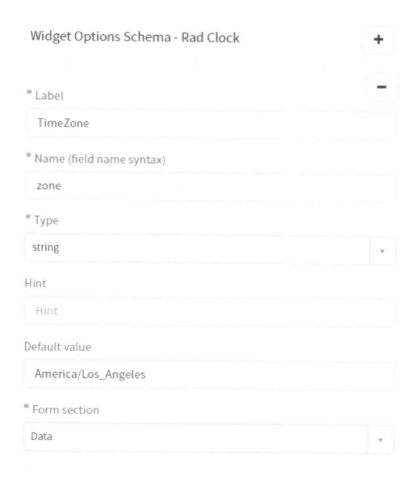

Option schema is unfortunately a drastically under-utilized feature of service portal widgets, but it is the best way to make the functionality you build with widgets modular, future-friendly, and "DRY" (D.R.Y.: Don't Repeat Yourself).

Once your option schema is defined, you can **CTRL+Right-click** a widget instance on a page and click **Instance options** in order to quickly modify the options for a specific instance of your widget.

Pro-tip: CTRL+Right-clicking a widget in a service portal page will show you the widget context menu for the particular widget, as well as an option to open the page *itself in the **Designer** tool, and to log $scope and $scope.data to the browser console, for easy troubleshooting!*

UPDATE MANAGEMENT

Get your development together.

UPDATE SETS are used to track, maintain, and deploy development changes – whether it's configuration, code, layouts, or anything else that's tracked in Update Sets. Once your changes are ready for deployment to another instance, Update Sets are also how you move your changes between instances. You can export them to XML (once the State is set to Complete) and import that XML into the target instance, or you can retrieve them from the target instance before previewing and deploying them. Whichever method you use, it's important to *sanitize* your Update Sets, keep them clean, and keep them functional. That's "functional" as in "functional programming".

In this chapter, we're going to learn about **batching**, **merging**, what is and **isn't** tracked in Update Sets, common pitfalls when dealing with scoped records, and how to correctly handle **preview** errors.

UPDATE SET BATCHING

ServiceNow released **Update Set batching** in the Jakarta release of the Now platform, allowing you to **group** Update Sets together in a logical hierarchical grouping. This enables you to preview and commit them in bulk, and in order.

Update Set batching takes a lot of the hassle and annoyance out of managing large groups of Update Sets for a major release, and allows you to extract a specific set of functionality from a release without impacting the rest. For example, consider a scenario where you need to do **A**, which enables you to do **B**, which enables you to then do **C**. If there's a problem with **B**, whoever does the deployment will have to be aware that **C** relies upon **B**, or the deployment of **C** will fail spectacularly!

"Dependencies" like this are a major issue, but also consider which of the records in your update sets might **reference** other records. For example, if you have a table which extends another table, you cannot push the **child** table before pushing the **parent** table, because the child references the parent table in order to inherit its fields and attributes.

Hierarchical Update Set batching makes this process easier, but is by no means a catch-all solution. You still have to **build**, **maintain**, and **control** the Update Set hierarchy and think carefully about where each Update Set belongs in the chain. Typically, the best-practice is to have the chain build chronologically, in order to avoid having a newer version of a record in a parent Update Set, and an older version of the record, in a child Update Set (which would result in an error).

If a child update set contains a record that also exists in one of the update sets that is "up-stream" from it, the version of that record in the child update set **must be newer** than the version in the parent set.

Pro-tip: Deploying an update set will cause a system cache flush, which can impact performance. It is often a good idea to deploy during lunch, or before or after business hours.

MASTER UPDATE SETS

It's not a bad idea to begin a release or large project by creating a "Master" Update Set in your dev environment. This is the Update Set under which all related "child" Update Sets will live. It's also good to have a naming convention that makes sense, but that's something your team will have to figure out internally to determine what works best. I'll use the name **Release April 2018-Master** as my example "master" Update Set.

No updates will actually go into the master Update Set. Instead, this will just be used to "contain" the Update Sets that contain any development that should be moved along as part of the "April 2018" release. Whenever a developer creates a new Update Set for some development, they'll set the **Parent** field on their Update Set to this master set.

As an example, imagine I've created two Update Sets for some development that I've been assigned stories for: **TW-Automate Inc Assignment-v1.0** and **TW-Build Catalog Item-v1.0**, and give them both helpful descriptions. I set these Update Sets' **Parent** field to **Release April 2018-Master**, since they're both scheduled for the April 2018 release, but if they needed to be pushed back at some point, I could give them a different parent. The master Update Set would not have a parent.

After identifying something additional that needs to be added, I create **TW-Build Catalog Item-v1.1**. This "1.1" Update Set will be a child of **TW-Build Catalog Item-v1.0** *rather than* **Release April 2018-Master**, since it is dependent directly on v1.0. This way, if the story to which they both relate needs to be moved back to the next release, I can just reassign v1.0, and v1.1 will come along with it. By making 1.1 the child of 1.0 rather than the child of the master set, I also ensure that the order of deployment is maintained, which is important because 1.1 will surely reference records contained within 1.0.

Let's have a look at what these relationships look like visually. You can click the **Visualize Update Set Batch** from any Update Set form, to see a visual representation of the relationships between your Update Sets and their hierarchy.

*Note: Right-clicking an Update Set in this view, and clicking **Prune**, will only prune it from that **view**. This does not actually prune the Update Set from the batch hierarchy. If you refresh the batch visualizer, the pruned Update Set will reappear.*

As you can see, from the master upset set, we split into two branches; but you can have as many child Update Sets as you like. If we then right-click on the master Update Set, and click **Edit**, we can see the **Child Update Sets** related list. This is a list of all of the Update Sets which are **immediate** children of the master set. It does not include the *children of the children* of the master set.

To see **all** of the Update Sets in the entire batch, go to the maser Update Set, and open the **Update Sets In Batch** related list.

Note: *Closing the master Update Set will close **all child Update Sets in the batch**. However, closing any child Update Set – even if it has children of its own – will not close any others in the batch, including its children.*

MERGING UPDATE SETS

Merging your Update Sets is advisable over batching in most scenarios where you're the only developer working on a given subset of functionality, because it provides a "safer" and more consistent deployment. That said, there's nothing wrong with batching to keep your Update Sets connected for tracking purposes, and then merging prior to deployment.

Batching is still a perfectly acceptable solution, especially when there are multiple developers working on a single project. You just have to be mindful of the "hierarchy" of the update sets in the batch.

WHAT IS AND ISN'T TRACKED

In ServiceNow, it's important to understand the difference between **data** and **configuration/customization**. Data is stuff that fills up tables.

Only what ServiceNow considers **configuration/customization** is captured in Update Sets, but it can sometimes be a little bit difficult to pin down what constitutes configuration without simply knowing in advance. For this reason, if you're not 100% certain that a particular record type is indeed captured in Update Sets, it's a good idea to open your Update Set in another tab, sort your updates by the *sys_updated* column, and make sure that your changes were captured.

Records which are not "captured" in Update Sets can still be forced into them. For example, if you want to force a specific record in the **Location** [cmn_location] table (which isn't tracked) into your Update Set, you can do so in a Background Script using the GlideUpdateManager2 API. In some cases, such as with a large number of records, it makes more sense just to export them all to XML and manually import them into the target instance after deploying your Update Set.

Pro-tip: To make it a little easier to include data records (since nearly every developer needs to do this quite often), you can download a tool I wrote, which puts a "Include in Update Set" button in the Related Links of every record and list context menu for every table that isn't tracked in Update Sets if you're an admin. You can find this free tool at http://updatetracker.snc.guru/!

While **not exhaustive**, here is a list of some of the records that are/aren't included in update sets. You might be surprised by some of the examples.

The following **are** tracked in Update Sets:
- Roles
- Form sections and layouts
- Reports
- Form and list views

The following are **not** tracked in Update Sets:
- Scheduled jobs & scheduled script executions
- Schedules
- Configuration Items
- Users
- Groups (and group *types*)
- Group memberships
- Role assignment (to users *or* groups)
- Homepages/Dashboards

You'll also find that there are certain records that are dependent on other records for their functionality. For example, if you create a role in the **Role** [sys_user_role] table, that will be tracked. If you then create a **group** (which isn't tracked), add the **role** to that group, and then force that group into your update set, you might be surprised to find that the roles you gave it **didn't come along with it**. This is because the associations between roles and groups is stored in the sys_group_has_role table which is also not tracked in update sets. Similarly, the association between **users** and roles is in the sys_user_has_role table, which is also not tracked in update sets.

There is a similar situation that happens with **dashboards**. Dashboards contain several linked *pieces* that are each not captured in update sets. Each new tab in the pa_tabs table is linked to two tables (sys_portal_page and sys_grid_canvas). To get dashboards into your update set, you have to grab each of those types of records.

PRIVATE SYSTEM PROPERTIES

One special case to be aware of, is **private System Properties** (that is, System Properties with the "**Private**" checkbox checked). These records *are* tracked in your Update Set, but when you go to deploy that Update Set in a target instance, you'll notice that the System Property is not actually created (if it doesn't already exist), and will not update the System Property if it does already exist in the target environment. This functionality is actually rather intentional, and is more "feature" than "bug", insofar as the whole purpose of the "**Private**" checkbox, is to prevent accidentally promoting System Properties containing data that is **instance-specific**. For example, imagine you've got a system property that controls which MID server to use for a given set of REST Methods, when invoked via script. You might very likely have different MID Servers for your development environment, than you do for your production environment. Therefore, you would want this property to be **private** so that when you set the property in dev, it doesn't accidentally get carried over to prod and overwrite the setting pointing to your production mid server.

Normally, this is a good thing. However, it's something that's important to be mindful of when – not updating but **creating** a System Property that's private. This is because on the target instance, the INSERT within your update set for a private System Property is completely ignored, just like an UPDATE to that System Property would be. This means that the *sys_properties* record would not even be created! Because of this, you must be mindful to do a few things:

1. Always make a "pre-deployment" and "post-deployment checklist", and include that checklist in your Update Set, to ensure that – among any other necessary steps – any private System Properties are created.
2. As mentioned in the System Properties section of the Configurability chapter in this book, always specify a "default value" (the second argument) for System Properties that aren't found, when calling `gs.getProperty()`.
3. Always practice **defensive programming** – *even against yourself*! In part, this means thinking about all of the ways that anything could possibly go wrong and checking for those issues in your code. For example, perhaps you can't reasonably specify a "default value" for a System Property, because you'd have no way to know an acceptable value if the property isn't set. In that case, specify a default value that is just a blank string (' '), and then have another couple lines of code that check for that like so:

```
var myProp = gs.getProperty('some_prop', '');
if (!myProp) { throw new Error('System property
"some_prop" not set.'); }5253
```

TRACKING SCOPED RECORDS

To be honest, working with Update Sets inside of scoped applications in ServiceNow can be a real bother. In this section, we'll go over a few specific rules to be aware of, to hopefully save you and your team some headaches.

For starters, it's important to understand that a single Update Set should never contain records from multiple application scopes. The platform tries to prevent this, but for some reason, it happens anyway. If at all possible, you want

---

[52] *Please note that unfortunately, ServiceNow's $Error$ constructor does not properly set the $lineNumber$ property of the $Error$ object. For this reason (and obviousl, others), it's a good idea to be very descriptive in your error messages if your use a $throw$ statement.*

Exceptions caught by ServiceNow's script processor will correctly set the $.lineNumber$ property, so if you put your code in a $try/catch$ block, and there is an error that you didn't manually $throw$, you'll be able to use that property in your error messaging to determine where exactly the error was.

[53] *The practice of detecting errors early and throwing or returning them, is called "failing early". This best-practice makes your code more clear and succinct, and also makes failure more apparent and performance-friendly. It also minimizes the potential negative externalities that may be caused by erroring code. For example, if your code updates a record or does a REST call or something before the error is detected, but the error prevents your code from continuing, you may be left with artefacts of all the work it did between the error being detectable, and being detected.*

Always aim to detect errors early, and – if they're show-stoppers – $throw$, halt, $continue$, or $return$ early!

to avoid it at all costs. Update Sets have a specific scope, and you cannot deploy updates in one scope using an Update Set in another scope.

There are plenty of scenarios where you may need to work within multiple scopes. For example, the **HR** application consists of multiple separate application scopes including **Human Resources: Core** and **Human Resources: Service Portal**. One development effort may require that you work with records in both HR scopes, as well as records in the Global scope. This typically requires manually creating **three separate Update Sets**: one for each scope. The Update Set you have selected persists when you switch back to a specific scope, but not between scopes.

For example, if you have **Update Set 1** selected in the **Human Resources: Core** scope, then you switch to the **Global** scope and select **Update Set 2**, and finally switch *back* to the **Human Resources: Core** scope, you'll find that you still have **Update Set 1** selected. This will persist until you change your Update Set *while in that scope*.

There are some additional headaches to contend with, too. For example: typically, when you visit a record that's in a different scope than your session is in, you cannot edit the record and you get a warning like this:

> 🛈 This record is in the Human Resources: Core application, but Global is the current application. To edit this record click here.

You can click the link at the end of that message to switch (for the duration of that one update) to the scope in which the record resides, but you won't be able to see what Update Set is selected in that scope unless you switch your whole session to the relevant scope.

Another reason to be very careful when dealing with scoped updates, is that some **tables** are in a certain scope, but the **records** in them are in a different scope. Again, ServiceNow is working on this, but when this happens, there is no good way to tell that you're effectively poisoning your Update Set with updates in multiple scopes, making it so it won't be able to be deployed.

For an example of this, consider the following steps:

1. Select the **Human Resources: Core** application
2. Create an Update Set in the **Human Resources: Core** application. Set it as your current Update Set.
3. Navigate to the **sn_hr_core_service** table.
4. Open any record in that table, and make any update to it, so the record is captured in your Update Set.

You'll notice that the record is tracked in your Update Set. However, in some instances, you'll also notice that even though the **sn_hr_core_service** table (like your Update Set) is in the **Human Resources: Core** scope, the update itself is in the **Global** scope. This Update Set cannot be deployed until all updates it contains are in the same scope that it's in.

Unfortunately, the only way around this right now when dealing with multiple scopes, is to double-check that any new updates you make are tracked in your Update Set, and in the correct scope.

Note: ServiceNow has been making an effort to patch this issue wherever they find it by updating the plugin, but they do not usually offer retroactive patches if you've already deployed a given scoped application or plugin. You might have some luck if you notice this issue in your instance, by opening a HI ticket (http://hi.servicenow.com/). The key is just to keep an eye on it to make sure your Update Set and update scopes match.

PROMOTION

Code promotion is obviously one of the most important processes you can have as a development team. I mean, you can write the best code in the world, but if it borks production because of a bad merge, nobody's going to be patting you on the back!

A robust code promotion process consists of a few key factors:

1. Is your **source instance** clean and (aside from the code you're promoting), relatively in-sync with the target instance?
    a. This question often comes down to asking yourself "when was the last time this instance was cloned over?" and "how much work has been started but not finished or abandoned in this environment, since the last clone?"
    b. See the upcoming Cloning section of this chapter for more info.
2. Is everything you intended to deploy, captured in your Update Sets?
    a. Review the section of this chapter on things that *are* and *are not* captured in Update Sets, and ensure everything you want to move is tracked.
    b. Do you have any private System Properties that need to be manually created in the target instance? As mentioned in the Private System Properties section of What is and Isn't Tracked, even if private System Properties appear in your Update Set, they may not be created in the target instance!
    c. Does your functionality rely on any **data** (records which aren't in a tracked table)? If so, make sure that these

records are manually pushed into your Update Set, using a tool such as my **"Include in Update Set"** tool (available for free, at https://include.snc.guru). Don't forget to make sure that you've got the **latest** version of every data record you intend to move over![54]

3. Are there any steps that need to be taken manually, **before** or **after** deployment in the target environment? If so, be sure to mention those steps in your Update Set description.

    a. It's important to have a standardized process of deployment which includes either reading Update Set descriptions, or otherwise ensuring that any necessary manual steps are taken on the target environment. This should be **firmly** a part of **any company's deployment strategy**!

4. If issues are identified in testing, **fix those issues in the dev environment** in a **new Update Set**, and push them up via an Update Set. You can batch or re-merge the Update Sets in Test once you're ready to promote, but never make changes directly in Test, except to facilitate testing; for example, by setting a System Property or following a Guided Setup to configure an application for testing – but be sure to do so in the Default Update Set so those changes aren't captured in what's promoted to production. And don't forget to make sure that the necessary set-up steps are captured somewhere!

CLONING

Cloning from your production environment over sub-prod environments like Dev or Test, is a very important step for any ServiceNow customer. In this section, we're going to learn some important best-practices for cloning, and discuss some suggestions for clone cadences (the frequency and process with which to clone your environments to minimize both instance drift, and downtime).

ServiceNow now lets administrators manage instance cloning much more fully from *within* your instance, using the **System Clone** application navigator modules[55]. Their documentation (see footnote) is actually quite good on this

---

[54] *Don't forget that if you manually push a record into your Update Set using a tool such as my **Include in Update Set** tool (https://include.snc.guru), and then modify that record, it's the **old** version that will still be captured in your Update Set! You must manually re-push the updated record into your Update Set. This applies for data records, and things like scheduled script executions and anything else not captured in Update Sets.*

topic, so I won't repeat what they say here, but I will point out a few important notes to be aware of.

First off, it's important to be aware of the fact that clones copy data from the **most recent *nightly backup* of the source instance**. So let's say you have a clone scheduled for Friday at Noon, but someone made or deployed a change to production on Friday morning (*boo!*). That change may not be captured in the clone, and you would end up with an already-drifted sub-prod instance!

It's also a good idea to keep in mind that if you try to clone *from* an instance running one version of ServiceNow, *over* an instance running another version, a central web service will automatically modify the target instance to match the version of ServiceNow that the source instance is running. This is normally desirable, but it should be noted that this process may take **up to 8 hours** to complete on top of the normal clone time! This process starts 8 hours **before** the scheduled clone time, so be sure to have any work or records you need backed up exported from the target instance at least 8 hours before the scheduled time of your clone!

CLONE CADENCES

The increasing differences between your production environment and sub-prod environments, is called **instance drift**. Instance drift is **bad**. The way to minimize instance drift, is to clone over your sub-prod instances (from production) on a regular basis. Cloning is one of the most important things you can do to ensure a clean deploy, healthy sub-prod environments, and to minimize the risk of carrying over artefacts of old or abandoned development.

It's important to have a well-defined clone cadence in order to prevent these issues. Among other things, your organization's clone cadence might be different depending on how many sub-prod instances you have. In this section, I'll outline some suggestions for potential clone cadences, depending on how many instances you have.

MULTI-DEV CLONE CADENCE

We'll start with what, in *my opinion*, is the optimal setup from a cost-vs-benefit perspective: **one production environment** (obviously), **one test environment**, and **two development environments** (*with potentially a third if you*

---

[55] *You can find complete documentation on ServiceNow's cloning setup and configuration process, here:*
  https://docs.servicenow.com/bundle/quebec-platform-administration/page/administer/managing-data/concept/c_SystemClone.html

have a large "citizen developer" population, so they can bork that environment without impacting your team's work). The two dev environments can be used alternately, switching from one to the other each sprint, and cloning each environment every *other* sprint.

This setup has several advantages:

1. Build new work for the current sprint in one environment, while the previous environment is retained (along with all work done in it).
   a. This is especially valuable if something was not captured in the proper Update Set, or was not captured at all (such as if someone forgot to push an important data record or the current version of a Scheduled Script Execution into their Update Set).
2. If a bug is identified in the previous sprint's work after the new sprint has started, the environment in which it was built still remains pristine. This allows you to fix that bug in the environment in which it was created, without risking carrying over work from the new sprint that isn't ready to be deployed yet.
   a. For example, imagine if in sprint 10 you built something involving a Script Include. After sprint 11 starts, a bug is identified that requires that that Script Include be modified. However, that SI is also already being modified for an enhancement to be included in sprint 11; but it isn't ready yet. If you had only a single dev environment, fixing this bug in a timely manner would be quite difficult! But, as long as you remember to apply the "fix" to the code in the environment that sprint 11 is being built in as well, it's much easier with two dev environments.
3. Allows clones to happen at the end of a sprint, rather than between sprints. This means less down-time while you wait for a clone to finish, before work can resume. This also allows you to do a clone between **every sprint**, ensuring the minimum possible **instance drift**.

To help you visualize instance drift as a function of time and the work being done in an instance, and to visualize the clone cadence I recommend with this setup, here is a step-by-step guide, with visualizations. Instance health will be represented by color (green being healthy, red indicating a greater quantity of "drift" from production) over time, from left to right.

Instance Health

To begin, let's start Sprint 1 in our Dev1 environment. Note that this means odd-numbered sprints will always be built in Dev1, and even-numbered sprints will always be done in Dev2. Here is a representation of our instance drift over time:

Note that Dev1 increases in drift over time throughout the sprint, but the Test environment only drifts at the end of the sprint, when work from Dev1 begins being deployed to it.

At the end of Sprint 1, we deploy Sprint 1's Update Sets to Test and then (after testing), to *both* Production, and Dev2. Afterward, we begin work on **Sprint 2** in **Dev2**.

Throughout Sprint 2, Dev2 drifts as work is done in it. Simultaneously, testing may be continuing in the Test environment, and fixes may be done in the Dev1 environment. At some point **during Sprint 2**, after Sprint 1 is deployed to production, the **Test and Dev1 environments** will be **cloned over**, in preparation for Sprint 3.

At the end of Sprint 2, we deploy Sprint 2's Update Sets to Test, and then to Production and the recently cloned Dev1 in preparation for Sprint 3.

From here on, we just lather, rinse, and repeat the same process, alternating between working in Dev1 for odd-numbered sprints, and Dev2 for even-numbered sprints.

SINGLE-DEV CLONE CADENCE

Working with a single Dev instance is slightly riskier and may lead to additional instance drift between clones (to avoid down-time between sprints) but can save some money and lends itself to an overall simpler approach to instance cloning. For a single dev environment, you've just got to choose how often you want to clone and stick to it.

Organizations with a single development environment tend to clone less frequently than those with multiple dev environments, but the trade-off for cloning less frequently (and thus suffering additional instance drift and associated risk) is that you get to avoid some down-time between sprints. Rather than waiting for a sprint to be complete, then waiting for testing to complete, waiting for production deployment, waiting for smoke testing, then scheduling a clone and waiting for that to finish as well before being able to begin each sprint, you may simply want to clone once per quarter, or once every 2-3 sprints for example.

If you clone only once every 3 sprints, that cuts your down-time down by 2/3rds as compared with cloning after each sprint. It's still not as efficient as having two development environments, but if you have a small dev team and don't want to spend the extra money for that second dev environment, this is a perfectly acceptable solution. It does, however, require a bit of additional diligence when it comes to being mindful of instance drift between clones, and being cognizant of what is and isn't yet in production (especially when doing bug-fixes for previous sprints).

FREE TOOLS & ARTICLES

Have you read the blog?

Just when I thought I was out, they pull me back in!
—Michael Corleone, The Godfather Pt. III

 n this section, I'm going to provide short-links to a mix of articles and free tools on various topics related to ServiceNow. You can read more or download some of the many scripts and pre-built tools, available for free on the blog.

All these tools are provided free of charge, and without ads, nags, or any nastiness like that. They're also mostly unprotected and/or in the global scope, so you can see and modify the code as you see fit.

I'll provide a short explanation of the articles and tools as we go along, but I encourage you to check out the blog archive at https://SNProTips.com/ and explore around the site at your leisure.

SMARTER UPDATE SETS

Update Sets are how you track and promote changes to your ServiceNow environment from one instance to another (for example, from Dev to Test, and then from Test to Prod). They're a great tool for keeping things orderly, but they don't always tie up into a neat little bow when you need them to - especially ever since the implementation of Application Scope.

If you work with scoped apps (such as the HR or Vulnerability apps, or a myriad of others), you've almost certainly run into custom development being done in a scoped Update Set, but somehow containing Global (or non-scoped, which are basically the same as Global) records, and you've undoubtedly seen the dreaded error message, telling you that you can't deploy an Update Set because it has updates from multiple scopes.

Or maybe you've built a Workflow in dev, checked it out, made some changes, published it, checked it out again, made some more changes, and then promoted it... but then - D'OH! - you realize you forgot to check the workflow back in before promoting your Update Set!

Or maybe you're in an environment that has a few super green ServiceNow developers, or at a company that's extremely liberal with granting the admin role, and you've had to clean up the mess after someone else renames or deletes the "Default" Update Set in Global or some other scope.

In my years as a ServiceNow admin, developer, and architect, I've seen all of those issues, and in each case, I've written a little script to save a little sanity, and make my life just a little bit easier by preventing these issues. This tool is a collection of all of that functionality, meant to save you some headaches that come with handling mishandled Update Sets.

Smarter Update Sets (SUS) handles, among other things, these situations:

1. Duplicate Update Set names
2. Update Sets containing checked-out Workflows
3. Accidental modifications to the "Default" Update Set

The Smarter Update Sets tool is available for free, at https://sus.snc.guru/.

JOURNAL REDACTOR

JournalRedactor can be used to redact or delete journal entries that may contain sensitive or private information, or customer PII.

Note: *Many organizations have legal requirements for data retention, and redaction (or especially deletion) may be the sort of thing that requires approval from your legal department. It is strongly recommended that you consult your legal department for your use-case before implementing this API in your organization, and possibly even limit the usage of this API to specific roles, depending on your company's legal obligations.*

The Journal Redactor is available for free, at http://redactor.snc.guru/, where you can also find API documentation and usage examples.

SET CATALOG VARIABLES VIA URL

This tool allows you to populate variables on a catalog item or record producer automatically, by simply using a custom URL.

There are a number of reasons why you might want to do this - for example, imagine you have a generic access request catalog item that lets you choose a group, enter the business justification, and request access to that group. If you also have a knowledge article like "how to get access to [some system]" which tells you to follow a process that involves filling out that access request form, and requesting to be added to a specific group, you might want to include a link that takes you directly to that catalog item, and **pre-populates** the relevant variable for you!

This tool is available for free, at https://urlvars.snc.guru/, where you can also find implementation instructions.

TIME-ZONE UTILS

Dealing with Time Zones in ServiceNow can be a real nightmare. The only documented way to set the time-zone of a GlideDateTime object, is the

.setTZ() method. Unfortunately, this method requires a "TimeZone" object be passed in, in order to set the time-zone.

What is a TimeZone object? It's an object that doesn't exist in JavaScript, and the only way to get hold of one using the ServiceNow API unfortunately appears to be to use gs.getSession().getTimeZone(), which just gets the current user's time-zone. If you want to know what time it is in a different time zone, *you're out of luck, chump*!

At least, you *were*. Sufficiently annoyed by this problem, I finally decided to write a tool to handle this for me, and now that I've been using (and testing) it for a while, I'm publishing it for all of you lovely folks.

Time-Zone Utils is available for free, at https://tz.snc.guru/, where you can also find a detailed explanation, and usage examples.

INCLUDE IN UPDATE SET

The *Include in Update Set* tool is rather straight-forward. It gives you a button you can click to force any record into your Update Set; however, unlike other more manual versions of this functionality, this tool doesn't require that you re-create the UI Action for every table you want it to show up on. Instead, the tool installs a UI Action that shows up on *every single record* that is *not already tracked in Update Sets.* No more guess-work!

The Include in Update Set tool is available for free, at https://include.snc.guru/.

CUSTOM CHROME ENGINES

How often have you wanted to do something like look up a record in a table by sys_id, look up a user by user_name, or jump straight to a table in ServiceNow just so you can run a query on it, but found yourself having to wait for the entire table to load, or having to navigate through several pages, waiting for each to load before you can get to the next?

For me, the answer is "multiple times, every single day ಠ_ಠ".

Therefore, I've made a video on how to use custom Google Chrome search engines to make this process incredibly simple! Below the video, you'll find some examples of useful "custom search engines" I've used in Chrome.

The article (and video) describing how to create your own custom Chrome engines for your ServiceNow instance(s), is available at https://customsearch.snc.guru/, where you'll also find a bunch of examples of custom Chrome engines that I recommend EVERYONE have set up!

(*By the way, don't forget to subscribe to the SN Pro Tips YouTube channel, at https://yt.snc.guru/!*)

SERVICENOW AS A CAREER

Starting a career within a new IT niche can be risky, but the potential rewards can be outstanding.

Maybe you're just starting out your career in IT Service Management development/administration/architecture, or maybe you're a veteran of the industry and you're looking for a change. Either way, in this article, we're going to discuss ServiceNow, ITSM, ITBM, and ITOM as a career-path. We're going to discuss:

- Some things you should consider when deciding on your career path
- Modules and specializations that are in high demand right now
- Building an ITSM-centric resume, and what to focus on
- ServiceNow certifications
- Interview Pro-Tips
- How to break into the industry without experience
- Salary negotiation and expectations
- Asking for a raise at your current job

ServiceNow admins, developers, and architects are in extraordinary demand, due in large part to the fact that ServiceNow is the fastest growing IT platform in the market, with almost triple the share of its competitors. This, and the ludicrous speed with which ServiceNow has obtained this market-share, has resulted in a strong demand for ServiceNow technical experts.

Whether you're looking to begin your ServiceNow/ITSM, ITBM or ITOM career, or you're already an ITSM veteran just looking for a change, we hope that this article is useful for helping you to grow your career!

This article can be found at https://career.snc.guru/.

EVENT-DRIVEN RECURSION

Scenario: You need to perform a very heavy scripted database operation in ServiceNow, on a very large number of records.

To do this all at once, would: (1) slow down your instance, and (2) take longer than the maximum allowable transaction time/sql count/etc. and (3) other bad stuff.
Each operation takes between 10 and 60 seconds because of the additional business logic that needs to run.
You can't optimize the operations, they're simply slow, and there's a lot of them.

Example: You need to reclassify 100,000 CIs from one class to another (a very heavy operation on a large number of records).

How do you handle this?
I've run into this scenario a lot, and in every team I've been on (which is a fair number), the go-to answer, is to run a **scheduled script** which does the operation on a batch (some specific number) of records at a certain interval.
But imagine if you have the job run every 10 minutes, and it deletes 20 records per run. You can imagine a scenario where the instance or scheduled job is particularly slow due to uncontrollable circumstances (such as the volume of integrations hitting the instance at that particular moment, or a discovery run happening simultaneously with the scheduled script). In this case, the job could take some amount of time longer than the average interval between jobs, in which case the jobs would begin to "pile up" and result in a sort of traffic jam that would both be inefficient, and be a massive drain on instance performance.
The way to do this safely, would be to figure out what is the longest amount of time you could imagine one "batch" taking, and then setting the scheduled job interval to a little bit more than that amount of time multiplied by the number of records per batch. For example, if you do a 20-record batch and each record takes between 10 and 60 seconds, you might want to run one batch every 12 or so minutes. However, if you need to update 100k records at a rate of 1 every 1.2 minutes, that is 120,000 minutes, or 83 days - nearly 3 months! (24 hours per day.) This might well be an unacceptable amount of time for these records to be in this sort of sys_class limbo.

So, for an operation like this, how can we make it the most efficient that it can be, without bogging down our instance?
The solution: **Event-driven recursion.**

You can find my article which details this method of event-driven recursion, at https://edr.snc.guru/.

CONCLUSION

Did you get the memo?

Wow, I learned so much. This book was great! In fact, I'm going to go rate it 5-stars on Amazon!
—*You, probably*

In this developer compendium, we have aimed to provide tips, tricks, guidelines, best-practices, and standards that can be applied in any environment with a positive result. If you're an architect or code reviewer, we hope that you'll have found some best-practices here that you can apply to your instance, and that you might consider distributing this book to your developers in order to improve the quality and time-to-production of their solutions. If you're a developer or administrator, we hope you'll keep this book around to refer back to and reference whenever you're not sure how to handle a situation we discussed in these pages.

We also hope that whether you're a new developer or a greybeard and senior architect, you feel like you've learned something from this developer's compendium. For free ServiceNow tools and more educational ServiceNow developer-oriented content, check out our website and blog over at http://snprotips.com/.

If you feel like we've missed anything, got anything wrong, or if you have some tips or guidelines you'd like to contribute, please email Tim@SNProTips.com. Any tips you contribute may end up in the next edition, and if you're the first person to point it out, you'll be credited as a contributor in the beginning of this book. You're also welcome to contact us using that email address if you have any questions, or if your company is looking for some ServiceNow architectural or development support!

Finally, thank you – dear reader – for buying this little developer's handbook. If you are so inclined, I humbly welcome you to leave a review on Amazon, GoodReads, or wherever else is convenient. I also welcome you to check out some of my other books, over at http://books.snc.guru/.